T0129053

Poetry & Social Studies For All

Benjamin Uriah Critchlow

Order this book online at www.trafford.com
or email orders@trafford.com

Most Trafford titles are also available at major online book retailers.

Printed in the United States of America.

ISBN: 978-1-4907-3481-1 (sc)
ISBN: 978-1-4907-3485-9 (hc)
ISBN: 978-1-4907-3482-8 (e)

Library of Congress Control Number: 2014907922

Trafford rev. 05/14/2014

 www.trafford.com

North America & international
toll-free: 1 888 232 4444 (USA & Canada)
fax: 812 355 4082

Dedications

This book honors those who have greatly influenced my life. The references that follow say it all.

My wife and our children deserve pride of place for such devotion, encouragement and kind optimism even as I wore their patience thin with my constant "Listen to this." Thanks for understanding.

Can I ever say thanks enough to my grandparents whom I knew from three months old until their deaths? Thanks for introducing me to the Eternal, to man, animals and nature. I know His everlasting arms have always enfolded me.

Then there are my parents: my father, mother and my step mom. From them I learned so much over the years. Thanks for every ounce of advice and kindness shown me during childhood and later.

My uncles and aunts were so caring and gave meaningful direction. That meant much over time. This first book says "thank-yous" are but small utterances for years of childhood examples.

To my siblings and my nieces and nephews your good wishes and kind thoughts are more than enough for all you have been to me for all these many years.

"It is the eyes that listen. It is the ears that hear." Words from JHT and NM still echo today as do the words of wisdom of extended family and friends especially my village teenage teammates, JG, MK and RJ.

I salute some of the greatest headmasters anyone can ever have, AT, CS, DP, FB, HM, KS and MJ.

I honor all of you with whom I ploughed the stairs as over the years we strove to mold young lives. Thank you AB, AL, AR, BF, BS, CB, CM, CP, CR, DB, DS, EW, FD, GG, GS, HM, IS, JM, JR, JS, KC, KS, LF, MA, MB, MC, MF, NH, OV, PB, PW, RD, RH, SB, SG, SK, TD, TH, TJ, VA, YM and ZS.

To my students for the joy teaching you gave me, I say a million thanks. I dedicate this especially to DR who, on my first day teaching, just a stripling, showed me your notebook as if to say, "Teaching is not that difficult." To all of you represented by AB, AM, AV, BA, BE, BQ, BS, BW, CA, CN, DA, DB, DC, DR, DW, EC, ER, FB, GP, HW, IB, IR, JD, JJ, JO, KM, LA, LM, LS, LW, MB, ML, MO, NM, PA, PB, PP, PT, RD, SE, SM, SN-W, TJ and VY, teaching you was worth it.

Finally, I dedicate this to my own primary and high school teachers, especially BSS, CD, CVRP, DS, EK, HPB, HS, JCC, RK, SR and most definitely to Miss ND whose words of kindness to the eleven year old boy from a village that had barely three hundred people, might even have been less since I knew everybody by name, on his first day in High School made high school easier from that day. Miss D, you didn't know what that meant to me.

Foreword

Writers do communicate varied messages to their readers. In this text, PASS for All, the writer deals with topics that he hopes will challenge the individual reader. All are free to react to each poem from their own viewpoints. As far as possible, they need to visualize the poet's intent 1 through their own eyes 2 that of any character the poet refers to 3 the possible time period of the poem 4 the factors that might have influenced the poet's writing of a particular poem and 5 the life experiences that might have been behind the poet's work. Because the writer deliberately chose these topics, a few might bring memories that readers might have buried. Hopefully, readers could view their understanding from another perspective. It is my hope that readers would come to the poems with an open mind to see what they can glean from the poet's own world view which might challenge theirs in one way or another.

Part 1 in this book talks about lessons of and from life. It challenges and addresses the matters we face and can come in contact with from time to time.

Part 2 deals with Literature and Social Studies. The writer groups topics to give the reader the opportunity to weigh and consider. To effectively use this book, all readers, including teachers, could follow the poet's grouping suggestions or create their own groups.

I trust all who read this book would be touched by what inspired me when I sat down to write.

Benjamin Uriah Critchlow.

Note to teachers: You can contact www.BUCritch.com to find out how to get the Teachers' Booklet which includes answers suggested by the poet. You will pay a nominal fee for this resource.

Part 1: Poetry with some Lessons from Life

1. Caution

Stanza 1

Be very careful. Think before you act
Has always been a smart sensible tact
For people everywhere to follow
For the boss or the lowly fellow
Speaking in anger is not such a smart way
For any leader to seriously avoid any fray
From day to week to month to year
Of future time none can ever swear
Words oughtn't to be any symptom of fear
So let wise speech show a head that's clear
And caution guide our mouth year by year

Stanza 2

A thrown boomerang comes back to the hand
Like a word once spoken can affect any stand
Caution demands wisdom should lead the way
As everyone works hard to succeed every day
Regret heals little; hurt's never been much fun
The wise knows not everything is always won
Ofttimes 'tis better to be quiet; bask in the sun
And take time to think of the race not yet run
For since time goes by so swiftly each day
People could be at a loss if at work or play
Bridging gaps is a laudable act indeed
Once others appreciate that same need
So let wise speech show a head that's clear
And caution guide our mouth year by year

Answer all questions based on the poem, **Caution**.

1. What proverb means almost the same as "Think before you act?"
2. State the word, phrase or sentence that means the same or nearly the same as these used in the passage: 1 tact 2 sensible 3 fray 4 follow 5 superior 6 seriously 7 avoid 8 swear 9 stand 10 symptom 11 caution 12 guide 13 boomerang 14 affect 15 stand 16 wisdom

3

17 regret 18 hurt 19 fun 20 wise 21 bask 22 race 23 loss 24
laudable 25 appreciate 26 same 27 clear 28 need

3. How does the poet connect actions and words?
4. Why does the poet refer to the link between speech and war on the
   one hand and the two and future on the other hand?
5. (a) In what way can words lead to both 'fray' and 'fear'?
   (b) What are some suggestions made by the poet about (5a)?
6. Why does the poet have these two lines:
   "So let wise speech show a head that's clear
   And caution guide our mouth year by year" at the end each stanza?
7. What is a "boomerang"? How does it compare to one's speaking?
8. What is the poet's main advice to speakers?

2. Introspection

In every one of us is the hope to be better
Never do we think that we cannot prosper
The times that we do falter are ever there
Regardless of dreams there is always fear
To overcome challenges and face each day
Is our task to always tackle come what may
People must look inside to know what's new
Enquiring within will give each of us a view
To know what is inside us, who we really are
Is what we ought to grasp if we're near or far
Inside clearly are ourselves that we need to know
The new vistas and areas that will help us to grow

Answer the following questions based on the above poem, **Introspection**.

1. In two to three sentences write what you think is the writer's aim in writing the poem "Introspection"?
2. What does the poet suggest links each of us to others?
3. Why does the poet seem to be "forward-looking"?
4. What is the meaning of each of the words or phrases as used in the poem? 1 grasp 2 regardless 3 areas 4 falter 5 regardless 6 hope 7 face 8 tackle 9 vistas 10 prosper
5. Quote from the poem why the writer called the poem "Introspection."

3. Decide

This or that
To go or to stay
To sleep or to remain awake
What to choose or what to refuse
Like a little lad not sure which toy to use
Like a little lass not sure
Whether to sit near to grandma or grandpa
Decision walks among us
Like a parasite sticking
Unwillingly detaching
Itself from its host
By forcible extraction which ends the link
Totally
Finally
As time ticks
And the pitter patter continues
And everything is detailed:
Failure and Success
Life and Death
Joy and Happiness
Decision demands a resolution
Decision does determine destiny

Answer the following questions based on the poem, **Decide.**

1. In between three to ten sentences state what the poet is conveying to the reader.
2. Read the poem and identify different examples of figurative language.
3. (a) Why does the poet use opposites? (b) Explain to what extent his strategy works or fails.
4. What would be another title for this poem? Why?
5. (a) What reason, if any, does the poet give for the last line of the poem? (b) State your own feeling about that last line.
6. Which of the poet's comparisons of Decision to something else is most accurate? Why?

4. Victory versus Defeat

Yes! Yes! Yes!
It's over
The end of a struggle
Its over
The hard fought battle
It's over
As the last shot failed
As the last second passed
Yes! We knew it
It's over
Victory at last
Like the hunter savoring its prey
Like the hurricane sweeping through the city
The pent up emotions gushed forth
All there: the tears, the shouts, the hugs
Eyes cast upward, eyes looking downward
Tell the tale of success and failure
Joy and sadness, hope and despair
Of failed effort
Of odds overcome
Yes! One will bask in the glow
The other must try again and only hope

Answer all the questions based on the poem, **Victory versus Defeat.**

1. What is the poet's main talking point?
2. Do you think the repetitions help the poem? Why? Why not?
3. Pick out similes from the poem and explain them.
4. In one paragraph write what you think took place in the poem.
5. From the poem pick examples of antonyms.
6. What is suggested by 1 end of a struggle 2 the last shot 3 the last second 4 at last 5 pent up emotions 6 eyes cast upward, eyes looking downward 7 bask in the glow

5. Love sets its sight

Love sets its sight on what's worth loving
For love never would by itself dare exist.
It breathes and thrives itself in its giving
And thus for much attention does persist.
O do not spurn it!
It can stand no taunting.
Do not let it pine thus away.
For it must needs be left to yearning,
Searching, hoping, wanting to give itself away.
Why dare you refuse to yield to its pleading?
Your lack of it will leave you needing
A heart to treasure and to care
For if you can but be yielding,
Love's joys ever will be near.

Answer the questions based on the poem, **Love sets its sight**.

1. In what other century would you say this poem could have been possibly written and why?
2. Read the poem through and write a summary of between 5-8 sentences on its meaning as you see it.
3. Why is it possible that the writer might have summed up the major 'thrust' of the poem in the first and last two lines?
4. The poet makes a few assumptions about love. List at least 5 of them.
5. Why do you think these assumptions made by the poet are meaningful?
6. Why is it possible that because one's opinion on love might be influenced by the sum total of one's life experiences, the poem can be judged as both right and wrong?
7. Give your first impression of this poem in no more than five sentences.
8. Give the meanings of the following words as used in the poem: 1 taunting 2 spurn 3 pine 4 yielding 5 treasure 6 dare 7 pleading 8 lack 9 needing 10 persist 11 needs 12 thrives

6. Valentine's Day History

Valentinus or Valentine, historical legends said
Ignored Emperor Claudius' edict and was dead
He felt young soldiers' love should not be denied
He married young sweethearts and the law defied
Another Valentine, many still truly believed,
Aided Christians, Rome's justice he deceived.
Some say a Valentine died on the Ides of February
He's whom we celebrate—love treasured by many
Pope Gelasius declared February 14, St. Valentine's Day
Little did he know his edict would inspire romantic sway
Those who knew that it was the birds mating season
In France and England, found just about every reason
To celebrate over and over, again and again
Love's joys forever-what a wonderful refrain!
Bouquets of roses, red or of any other hue
Are generally gifted to lovers as if on cue
Later sweets and chocolate joined the lovers' scene
"Valentine" became lovers' day—so it has ever been
Cards, songs and poems were an important part too
Of lovers' celebrating people including me and you
It's true that many in every different clime and time
Ask only one question: "Will you be my Valentine?"

Answer all questions based on this poem, **Valentine's Day History**.

1. How many Valentines are mentioned in this poem?
2. State what made each Valentine different.
3. How did Emperor Claudius' edict fit into the idea of celebrating Valentine's Day?
4. Why did Valentine really defy that law?
5. What caused the second Valentine to deceive Roman justice?
6. Why is Valentine's Day celebrated on February 14?
7. Why was celebrating around February 14 easily acceptable to both the French and British?

8. How did they celebrate Valentine's Day at the beginning? How is it celebrated now?
9. Give the meaning of these words or phrases as used in the poem: 1 edict 2 historical legends 3 sweethearts 4 defied 5 deceived 6 refrain 7 hue 8 scene

7. Wishing hope would remain

Yes!
'Twas good to feel the cool in my face
Hear the echo of the words in my heart
Know that he cares
If only
If only it had lasted
If only promises were not broken
Words spoken had depth of meaning
And he was true
If only
Alas, like all the others who promised
But never delivered
Like Judas who betrayed Him whom eleven others loved
He failed me, betrayed me, bartered me
For younger eyes, firmer flesh
Yet I will not mope
I will not groan
Fifty summers have taught
That with life there still is hope.

Answer all questions based on the poem, **Wishing hope would remain**.

1. What do you think is the sex of the person speaking in the poem?
2. Give the person in question 1 an age range.
3. Why do you think this poem was written?
4. In one paragraph state the main points of the poem.
5. In the poem "If only . . ." is used four times. Explain what the poet could have meant by the use of "If only . . ." those four times.
6. Pick out any figure of speech from the poem and explain it.
7. Give as far as you can words that mean almost the same as the words following: 1 echo 2 lasted 3 depth 4 delivered 5 bartered 6 mope 7 groan
8. What did the poet mean by "Yes" in line 1 and "Alas" in line 11?

8. What a relationship!

Before we knew it, we were growing apart
The pain did shatter each individual's heart
No peace was left and no piece to patch
Despair on each heart had left a scratch
To think it was not that very long ago
She was my love and I'd let her know
Undying love we had to give
If only Ben, our boy, did live
Once we got swallowed by tragedy
Hope deserted. We felt very guilty
Yet we both played the blame game
And we lost our way; what a shame
But now thanks to Ben's memory
We have restored our camaraderie
Knowing our true feelings we cannot hide
Since love has won out over foolish pride

Answer these questions on the above poem, **What a relationship!**

1. Why were the persons, in this poem, almost separated from the outset?
2. Identify and explain examples of homonyms from the poem.
3. What do these words mean 1 shatter 2 blame 3 despair 4 camaraderie
4. What message does a poem like this send to people in a "relationship"?
5. Is this poem referring to a challenge for relationships? Why? Why not?
6. Explain the one thing the poet states that will help people in relationships.

Hope for Change
in Attitude

9. Dream On

Stanza 1
When trials come and nothing seems to go your way
Follow Your Dreams
When simple things seem so hard today or everyday
Follow Your Dreams
When doubts arise and fears hold sway
Distress replaces so much joy each day
Hope does seem lost; struggle's a breath away
Hold on; hold on; all dreams are meant to stay

Stanza 2
When friends desert, your days seem very dark
Follow Your Dreams
When families forsake, your future is very stark
Follow Your Dreams
When those you depend on, all seem to depart
There's one way to go; your dream is the start
Do not cry in despair; don't give up at all
Dream on in hope; just pick up every ball

Stanza 3
With your future before you, your hope is really alive
Follow Your Dreams
With the chance to be victorious, you just must strive
Follow Your Dreams
When challenges come, it should never be too late
If you look at the big picture, work, don't hesitate
No one's been victorious; no one has won the war
By following a leader whose dreams do not go far
Look up to the skies, let your dreams multiply
When visions are present, do not pass them by
Look to your future; let the constant cry still be
"My dreams are my hope. They are my destiny."

Answer the following questions based on the poem, **Dream On.**

1. In Stanza 1, the poet refers to challenges that an individual can face. What is the poet's suggestion about dealing with them?
2. Explain how the poet's challenges in stanza 2 differ from those in Stanza 1.
3. How and why does the poet seemingly change his approach in Stanza 3?
4. Would you call this poem one of expectation or hopeless resignation? Why? Why not?
5. **Vocabulary:** From the poem find words that mean the same or nearly the same as the ones in this list 1 there 2 ignore 3 shout 4 increase 5 loiter 6 successful 7 believe 8 confidences 9 opportunity 10 hopelessness
6. Find examples of synonyms and, or, antonyms from the poem.
7. If you were to give another name to the poem, what would it be and why?
8. Consider the entire poem and in one sentence for each stanza, state what each stanza is about.
9. Why does the poet make use of repetition in this poem?
10. (a) Is the name of this poem appropriate? (b) If you could, what name would you give it? (c) Why?

10. Future Longing: Hopefully All Get It

O for the revival of the talented tenth
The ones who yearn to learn to be sent
Not just to play or to entertain or soar
In the NBA, MLB, NFL, or PGA tour
This would have surely answered many a prayer
And engender in all groups an avenue to prosper
Not a hit or a miss in different sports alone
Or a hope and a prayer in the films to moan
Not in raps so many young women to shame
As in the videos their wiggle is all the same
Not as stand up comics that shout aloud
Debasing history to pump up the crowd
While young men wear their sags with such pride
As if undergarments they never ever should hide
While their lips drip a long tirade of cusses
Making one cringe about the alphabet's uses
Now discipline seems a thing of the distant past
Families' eating together's only in a film's cast
Maybe one day the truth will impress all and sundry
That a really educated citizenry's best for any country
For while sport has its place to help many relax
A surfeit of it can make one a little too lax
And we can't be demanding any form of innovation
With an overindulgence in entertainment addiction
As technical education has become an excuse for plagiarism
For it's easier to copy than plod through an entirely new prism
For invention still takes time-much trial and error
And still calls for much talent, much work and fervor.
To make matters worse these are not really jokes
But some young ones text in their resumes to folks
They can't waste time to type stuff that's long
After all any Godfather will right any wrong
It's just a job they want, see, it's no big deal
After all times change; ready to remake the wheel?
So when access to computer is the patented excuse
And many ignore discipline or branded it abuse

A value of Education can be lost in a jiffy
Because few demand inventive creativity
So time is now here for the new Talented Tenth
A brilliant group who will say yes to being sent

Answer all questions based on the poem, **Hopefully, All Get It**.

1. Research "The Talented tenth." Why do you think in our world today the idea of producing the Talented Tenth across color lines makes sense?
2. Why does the poet call this idea of "the talented tenth" a revival?
3. What is the poet's attitude to "sags"?
4. What two other types of behavior annoy the poet?
5. What is the poet's real feeling of the different players in the various leagues?
6. Which two sports have both male and female leagues?
7. Give the poet's three words and the two sports they refer to.
8. State the poet's unflattering observations of both young men and young women.
9. What possible lesson do we learn from the fact of young people's texting their resumes?
10. State the poet's "two attitudes to discipline."
11. What might the poet be suggesting when he says, "After all any Godfather will right any wrong."
12. **Vocabulary:** Give the meanings of these words or phrases as used in the poem: 1 the revival of 2 yearn to learn 3 soar 4 engender in all groups 5 a hit or a miss 6 an avenue to prosper 7 a hope and a prayer 8 a long tirade of cusses 9 lax 10 fervor 10 Debasing history to pump up the crowd 11 wiggle 12 cringe 13 all and sundry 14 surfeit 15 patented 16 inventive creativity 17 in a jiffy 18 overindulgence

Poetry and Social Studies (PASS)

11. In honor of the Nation: E Pluribus Unum

Stanza 1
Don't call me
Red Man or
Brown Man or
Black Man or
White Man or
Yellow Man
For I am
One Man
In One Land
One People
Recognizably diverse
But
In Same Land
All American

Stanza 2
By
Land Bridge
By
Boat
By
Plane
By Car or Tunnel or Train
From Steppe or Pampas or Rupununi
From Liffey or Kasikaitu or Erie
From Angel or Toco or Guernsey
From Victoria or Kaieteur or Mali
All Came
Shaped By War
Framed through Time—Land Forged Through Blood
Of Man and Woman too
She-whether our Grand-mother
Or our Mother-oftentimes
So young, and single, and
Often Abandoned,

Wife or Sister or Aunt
Our Womenfolk
Our Real Home Makers
Heart and Soul of a Nation
Of
One People
All American

Stanza 3
One multicultural Family
Celebrating
Rosh Hashanah and Passover
Mardi gras and Mashramani
J'ouvert or Carnival and Crop Over
Diwali or Phagwah
Ramadan or Eid-ul-Adha
Cinco de Mayo
Saint Patrick
Fourth July
Christmas or Boxing Day
Ganjitsu or
Chinese New Year's Day
Being atheist or agnostic or one of faith
Leaves no place for inveterate hate
Among a people
Following the teachings of
Buddha or Confucius
Reading the Quran
Or the Upanishads
Or the Vedas
Or The Bhagavad Gita
Or The Torah
Or The Bible
In its varied translations
Or The Book of Mormon
Or The Divine Principle
Or seeking to live like Jesus
A People maybe
Worshipping, Praying, Rejoicing

At Different Times
With Different Songs and Dances
Different Religions
In One Land
America

Stanza 4
Whether
French or Korean
Hebrew or Haitian
Krio or Saramaccan
Polish or Italian
Tamil or Russian
Swahili or Portuguese
Spanish or Japanese
Bengali or Chinese
Kwéyòl or Cantonese
Different Culture
Different Customs
Different Language
Man or Woman
Boy or Girl
Living and playing
Studying together
As a nation of one people
Different but still
In One Place: America

Stanza 5
Actor, Senator, Teacher or Writer
Chimney Sweeper or Elevator Repairer
Congressional Representative or Boxer
Sanitation Engineer or Scholar
Student or Construction Worker
Designer, Seamstress or Tailor
Pundit, Reverend or Pastor
Imam, Bishop or Preacher
President, Nurse or Doctor
Different People

Different Job
No talk of caste or class
As we work as one
Shaking off the stigma of race
We're one People
In this our one place
Our one nation
America.

Stanza 6
Whether playing
Association football also called Soccer
Cricket or Baseball or Lawn Tennis
Netball or Table Tennis
Rounders or Circle Tennis
Hockey or Squash or Rugby
Or Australian Rules Football
Or NFL or American Rules Football
Volleyball or Basketball
Remembering
Alvarez or Amar or Chavez or Lincoln
Drew or King or McCoy or Washington
Carver or Hiawatha or Kalpana or Walker
Geronimo or Huerta or Morgan or Latimer
Enjoying Calypso or Chutney or Twist or
R & B or Jazz or Meringue or Macarena
Or dancing Tango or Salsa or Soca
Or Passé Doble or Reggae or Samba
Listening to
Sparrow, Fighter or Kitchener
Marley, Presley or Makeba
Houston, Jackson or Selena
Mohamed Rafi or Mala Sinha
Perry Como or Frank Sinatra
With different background
And Different taste
Yet, from many,
One People, One Nation
In our Singular Place of Plurality,

Our Country: The United States of America.

Answer the questions based on the poem, **E Pluribus Unum.**

Stanzas 1 and 2

1. Write a suitable topic for Stanza 1.
2. Explain the colors in Stanza 1.
3. (a) What are the main points in Stanza 2? (b) Why are there different methods?
4. What does each method or each place in Stanza 2 tell the reader?
5. What are the locations and, or, geographical differences of each of the places?
6. Put in similar geographical groups: 1 Alps 2 Chimborazo 3 Tuvalu 4 Laos 5 Pampas 6 Kaieteur 7 Albert 8 Ganges 9 Rhine 10 Eritrea 11 Rupununi 12 Grand 13 Comoros 14 Caspian Sea 15 Patmos 16 Liffey 17 Tanganyika 18 Kalahari 19 Kiel 20 Atacama 21 Hoi An 22 Pakaraima 23 Indus 24 Stockholm 25 Himalaya 26 Bequia 27 Titicaca 28 Tortola 29 Bolivia 30 Hwang Ho 31 Rhone 32 Zambezi 33 Madagascar 34 Steppe 35 Euphrates 36 Victoria 37 Seychelles 38 Yangtze 39 Rio de Janeiro 40 Nile 41 Kasikaitu 42 Erie 43 Angel 44 Baikal 45 Guernsey 46 Mali 47 Nipigon 48 Aruba 49 Serengeti 50 Roraima
7. Why does the poet refer to women as "our real homemakers"?

Stanzas 3 and 4

1. What is a festival? Can you name a festival from your **ancestral** country?
2. Bearing in mind the religions listed in Stanza 3, in what way should one group the festivals, holidays, or religious observances?
3. Question 2 suggests two lists in stanza 3. If there is a possible third list, what is that list about? Explain the list and state each member of it.
4. Explain the main topic of stanza 4 by stating 1 What the poet is referring to. 2 Identify each cultural or linguistic stream by naming the country or countries connected to each cultural or linguistic stream.

Stanzas 5 and 6

1. What is the major topic of Stanza 5?
2. Identify any list in Stanza 5 that shows similarity between or among members of that list.
3. Stanza 6 has four specific groups. Identify them and place each member in its specific group.

Vocabulary questions based on the entire poem

Below is a list of words lettered a-j. Following the first list is a second list of words. Choose at least <u>one</u> word from the second list that means the same (or nearly the same) as each lettered word in the first list.

The first list (a-l): **a.** recognizably **b.** diverse **c.** individually **d.** variety **e.** odds **f.** soul **g.** framed **h.** forged **i.** stigma **j.** together **k.** singular **l.** plurality

The second list (o-z) o. exceptional **p.** difference **q.** strength **r.** inspired **s.** many **t.** affected **u.** noticeably **v.** different **w.** singly **x.** difficulties **y.** united **z.** insult

Final Question: In the final stanza, 29 persons are mentioned. Identify each person and state each person's claim to fame, if any.

Facing Differences

12. Difference a Reality

Our world should work steadily to deal sensibly with diversity
For no longer should we ever hear of forms of racist tyranny
As we continue to negate hate, and difference we do tolerate
That truth we confront will initiate more of a stirring debate
Many nations like Bosnia, Kosovo, Rwanda and South Africa
Faced questions, about difference, that did make people suffer
This matter about South African difference was what met Mahatma
Later dealing with it as a South African leader did challenge Mandela
Most of the world's civil rights stories have only been partially told
For truths have been submerged and contributions placed on hold
We know all about Buxton's work for ending slavery
And Martin Luther King's odyssey for black equality
Mohandas Karamchand Gandhi is known for all his work in India
Yet as Mandela after him, he did meaningful work in South Africa
People quite rightly linked South Africa with the work of Mandela
Few know Gandhi's foray into social justice began in South Africa
While Mandela was rightly hailed a South African son of the soil
Do many know that Mahatma while there for liberty also did toil?
Both men clearly did not set out to seek for any fame
But eerily similarly both strove to end human shame
In Mahatma Gandhi's day the anti-Indian attitude that existed in Natal
Foreshadowed Apartheid's racial acts that to Madiba became so critical
And though Gandhiji at first used his legal skill as a letter writer
Like Nelson Mandela too he was an effective political organizer
In 1893 Gandhi's South African experience was insulting discrimination
All Madiba's homeland offered him were discrimination and humiliation
When Gandhi went against the British for South African Indian dignity
He had to face the determined British and South African white hostility
At first rejected by India's nationalist movement for a leadership position
In South Africa in 1903 Gandhi founded his newspaper, 'Indian Opinion'
Promoting the passive resistance philosophy and the Phoenix scheme near
Durban
He foreshadowed Mandela's future constant struggle for African self
determination
Fighting for minority civil rights in South Africa inspired these different
men's intent

In different generations when respect for others' rights to some was so inconvenient
While the time that they did do in jail was hardly comparable
The works of Madiba and Mahatma indicate what is possible
Mahatma Gandhi did not let religious difference cloud his judgment ``
As Madiba who saw forgiveness important to his nation's betterment
While Mohandas Gandhi gave up political power to stand on principle
Nelson Mandela served his one term as he felt only that was acceptable
Mahatma and Madiba saw difference as no reason not to get along
So they strove for their people's unity to make their nations strong

Answer the questions based on the poem, **Difference a Reality**.

1. What is the reason for the writer to stress Bosnia, South Africa, Kosovo and Rwanda?
2. What three words in the poem suggest the importance of appreciating others?
3. What two types of government are mentioned in the poem?
4. Give reasons why you would agree or disagree with the poem's title, "Difference a Reality."
5. What was the end result of Gandhi's being willing to acknowledge religious difference in his homeland? (You'll need to research to find this answer.)
6. Research and find how Mandela used forgiveness in an attempt to unite his country.
7. Explain how both Gandhi and Mandela fought for civil rights in South Africa.
8. Explain these two lines,
   "While Mohandas Gandhi gave up political power to stand on principle
   Nelson Mandela served his one term as he felt only that was acceptable" Make sure to give clear reasons for the actions of Gandhi and Mandela.
9. Give the meanings of these words or phrases as used in the poem?
   1 tolerate 2 grapple 3 inconvenient 4 acceptable 5 to stand on principle 6 cloud . . . judgment 7 foreshadowed 8 racist tyranny 9 initiate 10 truths submerged 11 contributions on hold 12 foray into social justice 13 passive resistance 14 sway 15 critical

10. Name the four "giants for freedom mentioned in the poem. Research and in the table below state their work, the time they strove for their causes, the results and when and how they died. You should put the information in the table below.

Name	DOB	Major struggle	Country or countries	Opponents	Result of struggle	Period of struggle	How life ended

11. In what way did both Gandhi's generation and Mandela's generation had to face the inconvenient truth of equal rights for all?
12. Write a paragraph of between 30-50 words about how to deal with difference from the lessons learned from the lives of Gandhi and Mandela.

13. It's Century 21, Look ahead.

Supposedly gone are the days of Ole Jim Crow
Yet some still speak of "Those people I know"
And few cabbies still don't stop if they see
Colored guys: those darker than you or me
Research often shows that Kasheema and Lashanda
Will still be waiting for a reply already sent to Greta
Then those who are so comfortable talking Holocaust
Say "get over it" if folks talk about US's slavery past
It's as if saying nothing will forever clear the air
Making the stench of racism finally disappear
But with terrorism's strike profiling has taken a turn
As other Americans have become victims of its scorn
Muslims have been targeted by many on any given day
As if all followers of Mohamed were in Al Qaeda's pay
After 9/11 Sikhs found their turbans became a liability
For many linked their headgear to Ayman Al Zawahiri
Asians, Middle Easterners and North Africans too
Became victims of ridicule—to them something new
'Tis a religious excuse that continually stirs the pot
Heated by many a racist zealot who's turned patriot
'Tis not subtle for only fools speak openly
About shades of color, crass acceptability
But race remains that awful elephant that's hiding plainly in the room
Waiting for an entire nation to send it to its inevitable destined doom
Still in this the 21st century there is so much hope
With its first non-white POTUS USA could cope
In confronting its past of racial acrimony
That affected nonwhites indiscriminately
We do celebrate all of our people of every race
Red, Brown, White, Black, Yellow: every face
We do applaud their successes all the time
Overwhelmed when something is not fine
But truth be told we take a really dim view
Of race's adverse effects on us of every hue

Answer all questions based on this poem, **It's Century 21, Look Ahead**.

1. What does the poet suggest by his use of the word, "Supposedly" in line 1?
2. What impression can anyone get when people speak about "Those people I know?"
3. Why do "few cabbies still don't stop if they see colored guys: those darker than you or me?"
4. If it is true that "research always shows that Kasheema and Lashanda will still be waiting for a reply already sent for Greta," what is the research implying? Why?
5. Give the poet's reasons for saying that some would be "so comfortable talking Holocaust" but "say "get over it" if folks talk about US's slavery past."
6. Why were Muslims at the receiving end of profiling after 9/11?
7. Why did Sikhs also suffer after 9/11?
8. In what way might the poet have linked racism and religion? Explain.
9. What does the poet see as the advantage of the first non-white POTUS?
10. Explain the last six lines of the poem.
11. Give a word nearest in meaning to each of these words or phrases or clauses used in the poem: 1 research 2 comfortable 3 past 4 stench 5 profiling 6 scorn 7 strike 8 hue 9 targeted 10 has taken a turn 11 on any given day 12 a liability 13 linked 14 ridicule 15 excuse 16 stirs the pot 17 zealot 18 subtlety 19 shades of color 20 crass 21 doom 22 acceptability 23 that . . . elephant in the room 24 cope 25 racial acrimony 26 celebrate 27 overwhelmed 28 take a . . . dim view 29 applaud their successes 30 affected nonwhites indiscriminately 31 race's adverse effects on us

Think the Middle Passage

14. Why should I remember?

Why should I remember
or even think about it?
I was NOT there
at that time
the time of slaves
the time of greed
and of human cattle
of ancestors selling ancestors
pawning morality for economy
I was NOT there
Why should I **really** remember
or even care for a month
that simply simmers with history's
myriad millions of deadly dark memories?
I was NOT there
when need for labour on demand
made the valuably vital Middle Passage
become frightfully fraught with death
when princes became paupers
I was NOT there
Why should **I** seek to remember
or even let my mind wander to a time
when Death was a preferred friend
of Hopeless Life?
I was NOT there
when child bereft of family
saw welcome Death as better to hated life
And, as a Descendant from that Passage
Should <u>I</u> not look for what was lost whether
link or land or ancestry?
After all, **I was NOT there**.
But I too was not there.
Who lost more? You or I?

Answer all questions based on the poem, **Why should I remember?**

1. Research and explain what the writer means by (a) human cattle (b) The Middle Passage (c) ancestors selling ancestors (d) pawning morality for economy

2. Explain what you think the following could refer to and why: (a) "Descendant from that passage" (b) "princes became paupers"

3. How was it possible for **link**, **land** and **ancestry** to be lost?

4. Who can "you" or "I" refer to at the end of the poem and why?

5. **Vocabulary:** What do these words mean? (a) greed (b) myriad (c) fraught (d) bereft (e) vital (g) wander (h) simmers

6. **Figurative Language** As best as you can, identify literary devices and techniques you find in this poem. Make any additional references to the poet's style in this poem.

7. What might the use of **I was NOT there** suggest about the poet's message?

Tragic Incidents

15. The day seventy three died (The downing of Cubana Flight 455)

The day was October six nineteen seventy six
The travelers on board were such a happy mix
CU 455 stopped in T&T on its way to Havana
The first port from GT an important stop over
In Trinidad the two murderers did come on
Ricardo and Lugo had their bomb, just one
In toothpaste they hid it; they hid it in there indeed
A bomb meant to make seventy three people bleed
From T&T Barbados was to be CU 455's next stop over
Followed by Jamaica before its last stop Havana in Cuba
Between stop two and stop three, the bomb took its toll
Down to their deaths went every teenage and older soul
At that time the cold war did flourish both near and far
Acts of political antagonism was also akin to a civil war
For East or West gave support to its own theoretical side
To maintain a level of influence they hope won't subside
Killed in the flower of youth who knows what could've been
Graduation, parenthood and old age would now never be seen
Yet truth be told this act should not have come as a shocker
Once he ousted Batista anti-Castro forces' rage didn't flounder
When the Bay of Pigs failed Fidel Castro from earth to dispatch
His opponents sought the most crippling forms of attack to hatch
So perceived pro-Castro sympathizers became fair game
It mattered not where they were from; it was all the same

Answer the following questions based on the poem, **"The day seventy three died"**

1. Vocabulary: Give the meaning of each phrase or clause as used in the poem. 1 a happy mix 2 an important stop over 3 the bombs took their toll 4 from earth to dispatch 5 killed in the flower of youth 6 Became fair game 7 rage didn't flounder 8 akin 9 hatch 10 crippling forms of attack 11 should not have come as a shocker
2. Using information from the poem, trace the path taken by CU455.

3. How did this act take place? Explain using information from the poem.
4. Those who planted the bomb did not die. What did they do to ensure they lived?
5. From the poem what do you think motivated the bombers?
6. Give the facts from the poem on the following: 1 Two things about the bomb 2 Why was it successfully easy for one to carry out a bombing of a plane at that time?
7. What countries are GT and T&T?
8. What world-wide reality of that time is referred to in the poem?
9. What historical event is clearly mentioned in the poem?
10. What historical event is implied?
11. After 9/11 what is the crashing of a plane for political reasons called?
12. In what way was the act done in this poem similar or different to 9/11?

9/11 POEMS

16. Nine Eleven Background

'Tis true, very true, most people would say
Bin Laden began as a supporter of the USA
When the USSR invaded neighboring Afghanistan
Bin Laden was firmly on the American bandwagon
He and his devoted brothers called the Mujahideen
Gave the Soviets hell and the USSR left the scene
The Taliban took control of their native land
They supervised the nation with an iron hand
Most girls were very often not allowed to go to school
Some say women were second class under Taliban rule
Meanwhile, Bin Laden did go back home to Saudi Arabia
To find Americans "deployed" by the sanctuaries of Allah
Medina and Mecca "desecrated" by many an Infidel
Was too much to swallow: it's just like being in hell
So Osama Bin Laden spoke out against it day after day
Was banned by his own king and went on his own way
When the leaders of Sudan allowed him there to stay
It seemed he had decided to turn his back on the USA
He helped in forming Al Qaeda, a thorn in America's side,
So that death constantly followed Americans far and wide
Bali, Kenya, Tanzania, Yemen, buildings and ships had hits
Terrorists singled out Americans with their "murderous kits"
Before that others had also made many attacks on Americans too
In Lebanon, at Lockerbie, on the Achille Lauro their aim was true
But it's clear on 9/11/01 Al Qaeda war really did declare
When it hijacked four passenger planes in skies over here
Two took out the Twin Towers, one crashed into the Pentagon
The fourth fearless passengers took over and brought it down
Through their definite very passionate hate and intense fury
Al Qaeda underlined the intent of the real, very real story
Osama Bin Laden, Ayman al Zawahiri, Khalid Sheik Mohamed et al
Were in the world's cross hairs and these terrorists had to take a fall
President George W. Bush was right that their work should never thrive
Bounties were put on the leaders' heads: each was wanted dead or alive
Whether it was in Tora Bora, Afghanistan, or in any border cave
It mattered not; each Al Qaeda leader was earmarked for a grave

The attack on America took around three thousand lives that day
And Al Qaeda accepted responsibility; they clearly had their say
From then the world's citizens' lives changed dramatically
As terrorism's threat took its toll on countries continuously
Traveling with care, people paid heed to security everywhere
Bombings in Madrid and London placed other nations in fear
While some terrorists were captured and a few others were felled
9/11 did bring to the very fore a culture of extreme constant dread
All these years later those important terror warnings still remain
"If you see something say something" is ingrained in each brain
With new challenges, some economic, in nations near and far
The world's citizens became tired of a seemingly endless war
For Americans, Iraq was by choice, Afghanistan by demand
As all knew after 9/11 America definitely needed to respond
Yet many will always ask if the USA really did gain
By its ramping up a war and killing Saddam Hussein
Still many years after 9/11, most people did vehemently agree
Iraqis and Afghanis must shape their own form of democracy
But ages in the future History with all the truth it could muster
Will explain the effects of Al Qaeda's hits on each Twin Tower
After the tragedy the world just couldn't ignore 24/7
America and the world had changed because of 9/11
When terror's truth's told with reminders of people's dread
Questions will be asked about how Bin Laden became dead
Relaxing for years, without a care, in Abbottabad, Pakistan
He felt certain that he had outwitted searchers in Afghanistan
Feeling secured as he hid from the world's reach in plain view
He was taken out by an American Navy Seals Team Six Crew.
For though he thought he could impose his will however he knew
Like Napoleon before him, he didn't envisage his own "Waterloo."

Answer these questions based on the poem, **Nine Eleven Background**.

1. What does the poet suggest that Ben Laden's fight against the Soviet Union meant?
2. If one were right to think that Ben Laden justified his anti-American stance based on his comparison between the USA and the USSR, what could the similarities be as implied in the poem?

3. USA and the USSR, what could the similarities be as implied in the poem?
4. On what grounds, if ever, can someone or a state (country) justify the killing of innocent civilians?
5. Why did the poet claim that women did not have it easy under the Taliban? Research and refer to an incident, in 2012, in Pakistan, which can use to support the poet's claim.
6. State the details from your own research about the events in Bali, Yemen, Kenya and Tanzania.
7. State how those events in Bali, Yemen, Kenya and Tanzania were similar to or different from those linked to Lockerbie, in Lebanon, and on the Achille Lauro.? Why? Why not?
8. From the poem detail or list major events that happened soon after 9/11.
9. Stat how the poet explain any changes in people's lifestyles after 9/11.
10. In the end of the poem the poet compares the end of Ben Laden to that of Napoleon. (a) In what way is this comparison appropriate? (b) If you think it isn't, explain your position.
11. Vocabulary Question: From the poem find the words that mean <u>nearly the same</u> as the words or phrases in Roman numerals i-xxv. i side ii positioned iii let iv exiled v positioned vi force vii in any way viii unbeliever ix up to date x price xi home xii shrines xiii clear iv killed xv satisfied xvi accept xvii permitted xviii disrespected xix embedded xx worry xxi claimed xxii institute xxiii effect xxiv attention xxv constant
12. List and give examples of literary techniques or devices used in this poem.
13. In your own words say what each phrase means: (a) on the . . . bandwagon (b) too much to swallow (c) a thorn in . . . side (d) singled out (e) a bounty was placed on (f) was earmarked for (g) take its toll on (h) pay heed to (i) impose his will (j) he didn't envisage a Waterloo

17. NINE ELEVEN

None knew that day would ever come
Instead all dreamed peace would drum on
Notwithstanding the baleful sounds of hate everywhere
Encroaching on nations in bombings year after year
Ere Al Qaeda were the Basques, Mau-Mau, Tamils, the IRA
Longing to be ever free from their masters' tyrannical sway
Extreme ways they too, without doubt, sometimes did use
Vehemently striving to rid themselves of perceived abuse
Except even when you think you're in the right, people will say
None that killed thousands of innocents opposed the right way

Answer the questions based on the poem **Nine Eleven**.

1. What is the poet suggesting in line 1? Why do you agree or disagree with his suggestion?
2. Line 2 suggests that the poet believed that everyone had an expectation. What was that expectation?
3. What is the meaning of "ere"? Explain what the poet means in line 5 by his using "ere"?
4. Research stating who 1, 2, 3 and 4 are, what country they are from and what they are known for: 1 The Basques Separatists 2 Mau-Mau 3 Tamil Tigers 4 The IRA
5. What are the similarities among these four groups?
6. What does the poet suggest by the last two lines in the poem? Do you think the poet's suggestion is correct? Why? Why not?
7. Vocabulary: Read the poem again and give the meaning of these words and phrases as used in the poem. 1 drum on 2 the baleful sounds of hate 3 encroaching on nations in bombings 4 their masters' tyrannical sway 5 perceived abuse 6 in the right 7 thousands of innocents

18. Heroes and 9/11

The morn was cool; it had no weather blight
Many longed to enjoy the day
With such a clear sky and sun shining bright
Many felt happy in some way
But Death's so dark terrible damnable sight
Full of malevolence galore did appear
He brought His hate and with such insight
Reigned down suffering and much fear
Sirens blew; bodies flew from storeys high above
And many wondered about the ones they did love
But without any thought of own life or limb
Firemen, policemen moved with faces grim
However, a dastardly deed done in full view
Brought out the best in people of every hue
Time and again many did strive hard to save
Every virtual stranger from a concrete grave
Made doubly terrible by falling debris
Hurled by airplanes: Hate's emissary
Three thousand people died that day
From US and countries farther away
Few jumped and died others were in awe
So steeped in all the horror that they saw
But others came out and ran right back in
Propelled at saving others trapped within
No rhyme or reason defined those actions that day
Extreme courage caused noble deeds to hold sway

Answer all questions based on the poem **Heroes and 9/11**.

1. **Vocabulary: Write down the words or phrases that mean the same or nearly the same of the words, phrases or clauses numbered 1-19:** 1 many longed to enjoy the day 2 no weather blight 3. Death's so dark terrible damnable sight 4 full of malevolence galore 5 Reigned down suffering and much fear 6 bodies flew from storeys high above 7 without any thought of own life or limb 8 people of every hue 9 time and again 10 virtual

strangers 11 hate's emissary 12 looked on in awe 13 so steeped in all the horror 14 propelled at saving others 15 no rhyme or reason 16 caused noble deeds to hold sway 17 extreme courage 18 defined . . . actions 19 made doubly terrible

2. Why did the incident come like a shock?
3. State how the poet explained the setting and the day's occurrence.
4. In what way did the poet show people's concern for others?
5. Which of the five senses was overemphasized by the poet? (b)Why was he right to do so?
6. Refer to the substance in the poem to support the idea that this is an accurate name for this poem.
7. Why is "extreme courage" a correct statement for people's responses on 9/11?
8. Poets tend to use figures of speech. Identify at least two examples of figurative language used in this poem.

19. The Years Later

The aching grief still lingers
Heartaches and sad sighs still remain
Enraged anger still stalks the land
Years do not help to quench that grief
Even words of hope rarely bring relief
And though Bin Laden paid the price
Riding airbuses is constant sacrifice
Since time and security's so firm demand
Lie like Damocles' sword above the land
And any suggested terrorist threat real or imagined
Triggers quick response from the brave or frightened
Eager to ensure that in spite of whatever the cost
Reclaimed freedom, to terrorism, wouldn't be lost.

Answer all questions based on this poem, **The Years Later**

1. What does the title of the poem suggest about the substance of the poem?
2. Why does the first stanza of the poem suggest that time is not always a healer of pain?
3. Why does the poet suggest that both anger and sadness are present in the country?
4. In Stanza 2, the poet refers to the effect of time and speech. How does time and speech compare to the effect of anger and sadness?
5. Why does the poet suggest that Bin Laden's death did little to affect the way most people were impacted by terrorism?
6. What does the poet imply by the stanza that spells "Later"?
7. **Vocabulary:** Give the meanings of these words or phrases as used in the poem: 1 Damocles' Sword 2 real or imagined 3 triggers 4 quick response 5 ensure 6 in spite of 7 whatever 8 aching grief 9 sad sighs 10 enraged 11 stalks 12 lingers 13 quench 14 relief 15 paid 16 price 17 constant 18 demand

Honoring People or Groups
Honoring American Presidents

20. Poem on the Presidents:
PartI: Presidents 1-25

Number One was a Revolutionary war hero who served two terms in all

His successor, US envoy to Great Britain, helped his nation to stand tall

Two helped draft the Declaration of Independence, as did **Number Three**

Both died on July 4, 1826, the Declaration's signing Fiftieth Anniversary

Three authored the draft of the DOI and oversaw the mapping of Western lands

Number Four, tried to fight against slavery, but had too much work on his hands

Four, the Pennsylvania CC baby, helped **Three** found The University of Virginia

President Number5, to curtail European influence near America, bought Florida

Six, **Two's** son, a great negotiator and leader of strategic planning proved to be

Seven felt citizens' voices should be heard, so he founded his Democratic Party

Eight couldn't survive the deep depression that took place during his only term

But still sought reelection. His initial performance the nation just didn't affirm

President Number 9 served for thirty days: the shortest time of them all

Felled by pneumonia, he didn't have time to answer his nation's real call

Nine died in office. **Ten** became the first VP elevated to the Presidency

In his one term, **10** signed a resolution annexing Texas into this country

11 was the driving force behind the Mexican War and more Western Expansion

12, military hero of two wars, after serving sixteen months, died in Washington

While **13** began trade with Japan his 1850 compromise aided the cause of slavery

Resulting in what he mostly feared: his having naught but a one term presidency

14 agreed with both the Gadsden Purchase and the Kansas-Nebraska Act

Yes, to Dred Scott's decision and Kansas's Union entry, wasn't a wise tact

15, diplomat, legislator, and public servant, was seen as a supporter of slavery

He lost much support from the North and was not reelected to the Presidency
Sixteen, touted the nation's greatest, saw keeping the union united as his call
Civil War raged. US's fate was in the balance. But **16's** hand wavered not at all
Yet hated because he wanted all people, including slaves in the nation, to save
President Number16 was quite summarily assassinated and sent to his grave
Seventeen who was the VP elevated to Chief Executive after **16's** demise
Was the Union's loyal Southern senator. **17** got Alaska for a small price
17, the first President impeached because he had overtly supported the South
By the beneficial reconstruction he imposed on them when Congress was out
Although freed from impeachment, it was clear that **17's** presidency was over
To right the ship, USA voted in **18,** the Civil War's Union Army Commander
Two-termer **18** was President when the transcontinental railroad was completed
But **18** did not run again, so **19,** who ended reconstruction, **Eighteen** succeeded.
Despite signs of prosperity, **19** wanted no second term so **Twenty** was elected
But four months later, after being shot, **20** was dead. He had been assassinated.
Twenty One became the fourth VP elevated to the Chief Executive's position
His major act as President was to aid in the civil service system's reformation
Twenty Two who also became **Twenty Four** hailed from New Jersey
He was the President who received from France, The Statue of Liberty
He won the popular vote not the 1888 Electoral College victory
That went to Number23 who with it got Presidential ascendancy
In office, **23** ignored how he got in; about that he took little note
Increased taxes and government spending cost him the 1892 vote
Number 24, who before was **22,** was America's President again
Completing a personal political turnaround all for the US's gain
Elected to two terms, **25** served one, winning a war and American Prestige
For being regarded as a world power was a status the US now did achieve
Having new possessions and annexing Hawaii, which became a state,
By **25's** assassination, the United States had already redefined its fate

Answer questions based on **Poem on the Presidents Part 1: 1-25**

1. Research and list in order, the first 25 US presidents, by number, name and the month or years they served.
2. Who were the two presidents who died on the same day? State the date and its significance.
3. Which president bought Florida? Why did he do it?
4. List the Present states that were not a part of the Union during the period of the first 25 presidents?
5. Which President found the Democratic Party?
6. Which Presidents between 1 and 25 died in office?
7. Which presidents were assassinated? Fill in the table below.

President	Assassin	When & Where	How	Who Succeeded

8. How did each successor fare or how well did each perform or what were their individual achievements? (Apart from the poem, you might need to research on your own to get all the facts you need.)
9. How many presidents mentioned in the poem served separate terms (not consecutive or back to back)? Using the poem, explain how this happened.
10. List the Presidents who had been actively involved in war. State the name of the president and the war or wars in which they were involved. (Your own research is necessary.)
11. The first 25 presidents spanned the period between 1776 and 1901. Write a paragraph comparing the period 1776-1800 and 1801-1901.
12. If you had a choice to live during one of these periods (1776-1800 or 1801-1901), which would you choose and why?
13. Why do people still believe President Number 16 was the best of all? Give reasons why he ranks above 1 and 3 or any other before or after him?
14. Which two presidents can we forgive for not doing much after their first inaugurations? Why?

15. Explain the following political terms from the poem (Research if you must.) 1 envoy to Great Britain 2 authored the draft of the DOI 3 oversaw the mapping of Western lands 4 to curtail European influence near America 5 the Gadsden Purchase 6 the Kansas-Nebraska Act 7 Dred Scott's decision 8 1850 compromise 9 when Congress was out 10 the transcontinental railroad 11 political turnaround 12 He won the voters' popularity not the 1888 electoral college victory (Explain what this means and give the most recent example when this happened.) 13 sought reelection

16. There are two references in the poem that talk about 1 annexing Texas and 2 annexing Hawaii. What are the facts linked to these two references?

17. **Vocabulary: Give the meanings of these words, phrases or clauses as they are used in the poem.** 1 served 2 successor 3 helped his nation to stand tall 4 anniversary 5 had too much work on his hands 6 the baby 7 found 8 a great negotiator 9 a leader of strategic planning 10 felled by 11 demise 12 citizens' voices should be heard 13 initial performance 12 felled by 13 elevated 14 answer his nation's call 15 the driving force behind 16 having naught but 17 wasn't a wise tact 18 touted 19 wavered not 20 overtly supported 21 to right the ship 22 hailed from 23 cost him the vote 24 affirm

21. Poem on the Presidents: Part 2: 26-34

By 1900, on the world, the nation was poised to make an impression
So it embraced **Number 25's VP** who proved to be a smart tactician
"I took Panama" was **26's** boast. With that two oceans would agree
But Nobel's call to **26** was due to the brokered Russo-Japan treaty
27 was one more Ohioan who as Chief Executive did sally forth
After the Presidency, **27** was Chief Justice of the Supreme Court
Japanese flowering cherry trees in Washington were in **27's** term
Number 28 sought to enshrine world peace in a meaningful form
28 influenced the UN predecessor, the League of Nations, into being
But World War Two's murderous mayhem ensured the concept's ruin
Number 29 was known more for many scandals than any great achievement
And his death while in office might have been more a gift than bereavement
Number 30 was a silent man. On **29's** death as VP he had automatic elevation
His main thrust was the reduction of government spending and cutting taxation
The President who succeeded that reticent one faced a very difficult situation
Since as President**, 31** met the initial potent charge of "The Great Depression"
Despite what he did, all he tried was greeted with intense dissatisfaction
That in the next presidential election, voters dumped his administration
Four—termer, Number32, fared better than predecessor, **Number 31,** ever did
For Federal Government's help to people of the Great Depression had no lid
Farm and work relief, Social Security, unemployment insurance were in his time
Plus the "Good Neighbor Policy" towards Latin America worked extremely fine
Though he did enter into World War Two after Japan's Pearl Harbor attack
USA's contributions did help the Allies withstand the Axis's blitzkrieg flak
32 died before the war ended. **Number 33** proved to be a worthy successor
Who bombed Hiroshima and Nagasaki to ensure World War Two was over
33 also put troops in South Korea to stop North Korean communist advance
President 34 did what he could for world peace to have a sliver of a chance
The Korean War over, **34** used SEATO to help stem Communism's tide
And in USA, his social welfare programs helped the poor make a stride
US Supreme Court said school segregation was not a constitutional rule
Thus **34** put federal troops in Arkansas to enforce the rule in high school
Then he initiated the construction of the US's Interstate Highways

Transporting the military and helping transcostal trade for all days
When that Supreme Allied Commander's final term was o'er
The US voters did something that they had never done before
They just did not stick to the usually expected same old script
They just did not stick with a protestant; they chose a Catholic

Answer all questions based on **Poem on the Presidents: Part 2: 26-34.**

1. List the names of the presidents in the table below.

Name of President	Period of Presidency	President who succeeded
26. Theodore Roosevelt	1901-1909	
27.		
28.		
29.		
30.		
31.		
32.		
33.		
34.		

2. When the President said "I took Panama" what did he mean?
3. Which two oceans would thank the President for Panama? Why?
4. A President was the head of two different arms of the US government. State when and how that happened.
5. Which president was influential in the formation of the League of Nations?
6. What was the purpose of the formation of the League of Nations? Why did the League of Nations fail?
7. Why was the 29th President not that successful?
8. What is the meaning of these words or phrases as used in the poem, **Poem on the Presidents: Part 2: 26-34** 1 poised 2 make an impression 3 embraced 4 boast 5 proved to be 6 the brokered . . . treaty 7 sally forth 8 enshrine 9 thrust 10 initial 11 automatic elevation 12 potent 13 intense dissatisfaction 14 chance 15 fared 16

predecessor 17 farm and work relief 18 withstand 19 the blitzkrieg 20 ensure 21 sliver 22 chance 23 enforce 24 make a stride 25 construction 26 tide 27 dumped

9. Why did President 31 fail in his reelection for President?
10. Find, if possible, examples of antonyms or synonyms or homonyms.
11. How did President 32 make a significant contribution to America's History?
12. Why did President 33 do the things he did in his period in office?
13. List the strategies # 34 followed. Why did he follow them?
14. How did Americans show they came of age when President # 34 left office?

22. Poem on the Presidents: Part 3: 35-44

With **34's** terms over, the PT boat hero of World War Two became **35**
Ideas about service and country didn't stop his assassination by age 45
35 wanted the space program to put Americans on the moon by 1969
He started the Peace Corps, supported civil rights; things were so fine
But **35** had The Bay of Pigs and Vietnam as components of a fray
He launched as the leader of the West to halt communism's sway
But Lee Harvey Oswald's bullet in Dallas left a devastatingly sad blot
America's shot at Camelot ended when President **Number35** got shot
In 1969 as **35** hoped Americans did place a US flag on the moon
But the space race against the USSR would not end anytime soon
VP of President35, Number36 did lead a good fight against poverty
Escalated Vietnam but ensured African Americans a form of dignity
Through the Voting Rights Act signed into law in Nineteen Sixty Five
African Americans still do have a say in keeping US Democracy alive
Number 36 with Vietnam's unpopularity sought not reelection
So **37** took his place winning in some ways a fortuitous election
Robert Kennedy had been assassinated while his popularity grew
So **37's** strategy and communist claims boosted his position anew
Later diplomatic overtures to China and USSR gave him a new image
But although he ended Vietnam Watergate spoiled his political visage
Thus instead of facing impeachment he resigned from the presidency
Heralding another first by having an unelected VP to run the country
38 was that VP who became President after Number **37's** resignation
38's memorable act was granting **37** a pardon for official indiscretion
USA promptly turned its back on him; it elected **39** the new President
But he only served one term despite having some sort of achievement
The Camp David Agreement and Energy Department couldn't save **39**
Gas and Iran crisis and Olympic boycott made **39's** popularity decline
He lost to **40** who, in 1980, pledged to give USA its new national glow
His "evil empire" salvo against the USSR was **40's decisive** first blow
At Brandenburg Gate he said it all, "Mr. Gorbachev, tear down this Wall"
Then the Strategic Defence Initiative did speed up USSR's ultimate fall
Even if Iran-Contra did leave many questions unanswered by The Gipper
'Twas not love for Maurice Bishop that made GIs go to "rescue" Grenada
He said, "Government was the problem," yet he tripled the USA's deficit
With tax cuts and many tax increases too that history's truth will exhibit

41 was President when USSR's Communism's end was complete
His promise about new taxes did make his term an unfulfilled feat
Limited by deficits, little revenue and Dems Congressional control
41 got the ADA and Clean Air Act Amendments—not his only goal
With an able cabinet, **41**built a large, diverse coalition not a minute too late
Prosecuted the Persian Gulf War and did run Saddam Hussein out of Kuwait
But in his reelection bid he lost out to the man from a place called "Hope"
He's been such a very slick politician with whom many just couldn't cope
Smart, intuitive was **42**, but he spoiled it all quite needlessly
By Oval office shenanigans that showed his lack of decency
A shut down that neutered the government was under his watch
As was the infantile impeachment ploy his opponents did hatch
Those blips on the political radar were definitely sure to fail
Because the accusers' morality was just as decadently stale
42 left a surplus, made help for the poor from being too broad
And influenced the Israelis and Palestinians to sign an accord
In the 2000 Presidential election **42's** VP the popular vote did win
But to the arguments of **43's** lawyers the Supreme Court caved in
Nine months into **41's son's** term the world changed dramatically
As Al Qaeda's terrorists left a calling card seen by all and sundry
The Twin Towers, the Pentagon, American planes had death blows
The Afghanis and the Iraqis later did suffer their own terrible woes
Even as **43's** "War on Terror" did rage on unabated for many years
"No Child Left Behind" caused some parents to have cautious fears
The housing bubble burst but the stimulus ensured banks didn't fail
But USA faced its challenge in ages with a change beyond the pale
The first African-American president of the Harvard Law Review,
Number 44, became the first non white President of the USA too
While the Nobel Peace Prize in October, 2009 seemed so premature
The Affordable Care Act will give health insurance to millions more
As the "Birther Controversy" spawned "The Back to Kenya" theme
Taking "country and government back" was the Tea Party's dream
44 supported marriage equality, education and immigration reform
So some states adopted Common Core as teachers' evaluative norm
44's election and reelection only sought to emphasize for all to see
Deep seated divisions that must be removed from USA, this country

Answer the following questions using information from the poem unless otherwise advised.

1. List the names of Presidents from 35-44 and state the years they served.
2. What was 35's major claim to fame before he became President?
3. Explain, each in a separate sentence, what the poet calls the achievements of President 35.
4. State what the poet calls the two 'blots' on 35's presidency and say why they might be called 'errors of judgment.'
5. Explain the connections of President 35 to Camelot and Dallas.
6. What were the two most meaningful achievements of President 36? (b) Why do you think so?
7. Give two reasons from the poem why President 37 won. (b) What was 37's failure?
8. How did 38 become President? (b) Why is he called the non-elected President?
9. Why did President 38 lose his chance to win the next Presidential election?
10. **Name** one thing that made President 39 popular and two things that made his popularity fall.
11. What made # **40** defeat # **39**?
12. What did 40 mean when he said, at the Brandenburg Gate, **"Mr. Gorbachev, tear down this Wall"**?
13. What was The Strategic Defence Initiative and how did it speed up USSR's ultimate fall?
14. What was the major flaw in #40's presidency?
15. Who was Maurice Bishop and why did GIs go to "rescue" Grenada?
16. What statement made by President Reagan (# 40) still resonates today and draws the distinction between liberals and conservatives?
17. In what way did #40's actions raise questions about his claims about government?
18. What were the main achievements of # 41 for America and for the world?
19. What other world-wide phenomenon marked the Presidency of # 41?
20. Write an opinion about the significance of the childhood home of President #42 and America's need when he became President?

21. State two unfortunate happenings during 42's presidency?
22. What can be regarded as victories of President # 42?
23. What did the poet suggest about those who brought articles of impeachment against resident# 42?
24. How did 43 become President?
25. Apart from 9/11, what are two significant important topic agendas during #43's presidency?
26. What were the two firsts of # 44?
27. What were the major oppositions to his being president?
28. **Vocabulary: Give what you believe comes closest to the meanings of these words or phrases as used in the poem: 1** components of a fray 2 escalated Vietnam 3 diplomatic overtures 4 spoiled his political visage 5 a pardon for official indiscretion 6 salvo 7 unfulfilled feat 8 diverse coalition 9 slick 10 intuitive 11 surplus 12 neutered the government 13 infantile impeachment 14. ploy 15 blips on the political radar 16 to sign an accord 17 all and sundry 18 unabated for many years 19 beyond the pale 20 the Nobel Peace Prize in October, 2009 seemed so premature 21 the "Birther Controversy" spawned "The Back to Kenya" theme 22 Deep seated divisions

23. The First Non-white President

He was first introduced to America in two thousand and four
When Kerry wanted to oust Bush and improve on Albert Gore
His keynote address, "One America," caught the nation's fancy
And many felt he'd have a great future in the Democratic Party
Yet when in 2007, he declared his candidacy for the presidency
None felt he stood a chance against President Clinton's Hillary
A Primary ad had questioned if he possessed the where-withal
"Was he ready to take the three in the morning telephone call?"
Iowa gave him a boost; he made inroads in many a primary
08/28/2008, he became the nominee of the Democratic Party
The Republican nominee was a well decorated national hero
Mc Cain was a "Hanoi Hilton guest" as Americans did know
A likeable senator he was and a very principled leader indeed
Admired by left and right who wished that he would succeed
But in 2000 he failed to get his party's presidential nomination
George W won; Mc Cain supported with Republican devotion
Barack Obama, Illinois State Junior Senator, was hardly known
But as Dem 2004 keynote speaker on national TV he was shown
When the Senate beckoned in 2006, Illinois made him their own
Then in 2008 he led the Dems due to speaking skills he did hone
GOP nominee, John Mc Cain, too hoped the next president to be
Hoping to solve Wall Street problems and improve the economy
However Presidential rival, Obama, was just as determined as he
The first major party minority nominee was sure to make history
O's cool shrewdness and expectancy caught the nation's fancy
Over time his stock rose at home and abroad quite effortlessly
To discredit him, his opponents raised questionable points of view
Saying he "palled around with terrorists," and "hated America too"
Others, too, continued to consistently advance their "birther" controversy
Donning the notion, trumpeting the query, "Was he really born in Hawaii?"
In few African American groups Obama found things were just as tough
For some in that community did question whether he was "black enough"
Some opponents called him a celebrity referring to the crowds he raised
Around Europe, wherever he went, he was just really generously praised
He's "the Antichrist; un-American, a secret Muslim" some screamed
Hid two decades in Wright's "liberation theology" church it seemed

So many felt McCain would trounce him; the neophyte was doomed
Despite his "plenty talk," he was not quite politically well groomed
The victim of the "Bradley Effect" others were sure he would be
Whites would talk support, but race would decide the presidency
But by eleven o'clock on November 4, 2008, it was convincingly over
The results declared USA's President-Elect as Barack Hussein Obama
Many attitudes changed: people became so intractable very soon thereafter
A GOP leader swore he'd be a one-term president come hell or high water
His agenda wouldn't matter; it wasn't important who'll benefit eventually
"Obama must fail" was policy for those possessed with political antipathy
On the other hand many showered his administration with excessive amity
Hoping for Health care, marriage rights and every possible form of equity
Wanting equal pay for women, the Lily Ledbetter Act, to be law in the land
As a step in completely removing all forms of discrimination on every hand
They looked for all students to have a fair chance to afford an education
Not to be fooled by unscrupulous lenders unconscionable loan elevation
They wanted a system to give students a chance to repay each student loan
So the nation would have the ability to develop latent talent right at home
Some longed for the addition of more women to the US Court Supreme
Others pictured young immigrants on track to live the American Dream
While they hoped, out came the Tea Party, to Dems and GOPers a threat
Such an "independent caucus" neither had ever expected to confront yet
Embracing its own agenda although with a very clear Conservative spin
The TP swore "to take back America," and end Obama's "socialist" grin
Some rallies were meaningful and substantive in their discussions
Others, overly crass, aimed at fuelling despicable racist passions
They'll teach the president a good lesson and all must be well aware
That the one thing they will surely do is to help to repeal Obamacare
TP wanted to keep government small and ensure no increase in taxes
Cut deficits, ease middle class pressure and end Wall Street rich fixes
Being Obama's biggest critics, the Tea Party proved its real worth
Its midterm-election wins restored GOP House power in some sort
Yet just when it seemed the status quo had taken a settled life
Out of nowhere came a stirring from a noisy bustling new hive
"Occupied Wall Street," without anyone's suspecting, just appeared
With strident noise they aimed to singe each one-per-center's beard
From city on to city they assailed the one-per-centers with scorn
Hurling constant ridicule at the rich, night, noon, evening and at morn
They blamed them for the world's financial collapse and wanted it to end

Reminding all, one-per-centers cared little, with boat loads of money to spend
Such massive crowds at different and varied cities they drew
That much vitriol was spewed at them as their numbers constantly grew
"Lazy envious parasites," they were, "who needed to go take a bath"
Though many were young, aptly qualified, and constantly jobs had sought
From Zuccotti Park their influence spread to cities far and wide
So some civic leaders used law enforcement to stop the swelling tide
Meanwhile, the world at large was undergoing some significant change
And in Arab nations, like Egypt and Libya, democracy came of age
Entrenched dictators were overthrown oh so very suddenly
Egyptian Hosni Mubarak and Libyan Muammar Gaddafi
Yet still at that time the European nations had to deal with their own terrain
The world could be plunged in more chaos without a settled Greece or Spain
Only time will tell how everything will eventually pan out
Whether the economy or human concern will staunch every tragic rout
However, when we think of President Obama and things that have befallen
Most Americans did applaud when Seal Team Six got Osama Ben Laden
So while about Barack Obama's first term people can agree or disagree
He'll forever be the first non-white President in America's history

Answer all questions based on the poem, **The First Non-white President.**

1. Why was it necessary for 'the first non-white President' to need a national introduction?
2. When and why did this introduction take place?
3. Why was the tenor of his message significant to his listeners?
4. Why did people believe that the speaker had a political future in the Democratic Party?
5. Why did people believe that the 'first non-white president' had little chance to win the Presidential Nomination in 2008?
6. What was the major question against Obama's candidacy?
7. According to the poet, what was the main advantage of his rival for the Presidency?
8. In what ways were the two nominees similar in intent?
9. Explain what happened for Obama between 2004 and before the elections of 2008. 10. What was regarded as one of Obama's greatest assets?
10. What were some of the accusations leveled against Obama?

11. What was the major accusation against Obama's becoming President of the US?
14. Why was Obama even criticized by some African American groups before the 2008 election?
15. What were some of the different names Obama was called during the 2008 Presidential campaign? Why was he called these names?
16. What reasons does the poet give why so many felt McCain would trounce Obama in the Presidential elections of 2008?
17. When was the Obama victory announced?
18. What indicated the changed attitudes after Senator Barack Obama was declared USA's President-Elect in 2008?
19. List 6 things that people wanted the Obama Administration to do.
20. What is meant by the following quotations: 1 palled around with terrorists 2 hated America too 3 black enough 4 Bradley effect 5 independent caucus 6 the Antichrist; un-American, a secret Muslim 7 liberation theology 8 to take back America and end Obama's socialist grin 9 to singe each one-per-center's beard
21. **Vocabulary**: Give the meaning of each of these words or phrases or clauses as used in the poem, **The First Non-white President**. 1 oust 2 keynote address 3 caught the nation's fancy 4 he declared his candidacy for the presidency 5 None felt he stood a chance 6 he possessed the where-withal 7 gave him a boost 8 he made inroads 9 he became the nominee of the Democratic Party 10 a well decorated national hero 11 Mc Cain was a "Hanoi Hilton guest" 12 a principled leader 13 Republican devotion 14 was hardly known 15 the Senate beckoned in 2006 16 shrewdness 17 Presidential rival 18 solve problems 19 speaking skills he did hone 20 over time 21 to discredit 22 caught nation's fancy 23 his stock rose 24 stock rose at home and abroad 25 questionable points of view 26 controversy 27 donning the notion 28 trumpeting the query 29 generously praised 30 trounce 31 neophyte 32 amity 33 not politically well groomed 34 intractable 35 political antipathy 36 human concern will staunch every tragic rout 37 come hell or high water 38 equity 39 latent talent 40 on track 41 much vitriol was spewed at them 42. Only time will tell how everything will eventually pan out.

24. Abe Lincoln's Gettysburg Refrain

Faced with the entire union to save
Abe Lincoln, like the rock of Gibraltar, stood firm. No quarter he gave
Whispers filtered about the battles both the North and the South had won
The President knew that many a mother lost a dutiful son
So at Gettysburg on that fateful day
His heart was exposed in all the things he did say
Clearly before him one thing stood out in all verity
United the states must be to remain as a vibrant entity
It was not about The North; it was not about The South.
It was the United States of America he wanted with nary a doubt
He was firm, firm, firm that the people's will will remain
So on that famed battlefield he coined his famous refrain
Which umpteen years after people have taken to heart
Hailing his ideal idea for the whole not a part
Democratic Government was of and for the people he said
By the people it will last because of the valiant living and dead.

Answer all questions based on the poem, **Abe Lincoln's Gettysburg Refrain**.

1. What seemed to have been President Lincoln's major concern or interest? (b) From the poem, quote the two lines that indicate this 'concern or interest of the president.
2. Why is President Lincoln compared to the Rock of Gibraltar?
3. Explain: 1 like the rock of Gibraltar, stood firm 2 no quarter he gave 3 have taken to heart 4 fateful day 5 umpteen years 6 ideal idea 7 the whole not a part 8 with nary a doubt 9 the valiant: living and dead 10 a vibrant entity 11 coined 12 whispers filtered 13 dutiful son 14 it will last 15 his heart was exposed
4. According to the poem what makes a Democracy last?
5. Which word or words best describe President Lincoln and why? 1 considerate 2 concerned 3 committed 4 dedicated 5 determined
6. Give examples of all stylistic devices the poet used to connect with the readers.

Honoring Women

25. Women and Worth

One belief is that man was the first made
From his side came woman to be his aid
But though second formed she proved to be
The best asset of man century after century
But will women ever really escape the influence of men?
Or are they destined to be in men's wake now like then?
The very word they're referred to connects them to man
Either they are wooed or woe to them or the womb man
From youth to age to men they are clearly progressively tied
The descriptiveness of their life events to men are simplified
In youth her monthly **men**strual cycles can hit her with a clout
In late forties, fifties and sixties, **men**opause can wear a girl out
In the past, she's been treated as an appendage
But now, she's seen as a shining star of our age
Wife, mother, daughter, sister, aunt, grandmother
Loving woman she ranks supreme over any other
Achieving greatness despite the evils of patriarchy
Her grace continually made her in demand aplenty
Women's contribution over the years no one can downsize
Many a man knows the worth of a wife who's so very wise
In ancient times her dowry did make many men rich
Especially those who had little or not a single stitch
Queen or president or governor or prime minister
Worldwide she's been outstanding over and over
From 1940, there have been fifty-seven female Prime Ministers
Seventeen Governors General and sixty one Presidential Leaders
Yet in some places men say her face none should see
Thinking her veil could hide her regal soul of dignity
But over time she's been a real source of stability
Enhancing humans with much prudent capability
In many a trying time in very difficult situations
She ensured much calm in bellicose negotiations
Instead of rooting for war at the very first chance
Women use caution to dictate how things advance
Some: Elizabeth1, Thatcher, Victoria and Boadicea
Made important decisions in times of grave danger

To stave off the possible suffering of an entire nation
Consistently, they acted boldly, not with trepidation
So when men floundered in various difficult situations
Women readily took up the mantle of their generations
Men ought to applaud their strides each and every day
Women's actions can affect families in a positive way

Answer all questions based on the poem, Women and Worth

1. In a paragraph of between 3-5 sentences state what the poet is stressing in the poem.
2. Explain, if you can the three words attached by the poet to man to form woman: woo, woe and womb.
3. Why does the poet call a woman, "man's greatest asset century after century?"
4. How are the words "appendage," and "patriarchy," and the idea of a woman's wearing of a veil linked?
5. Why have women worn veils?
6. From where did the idea in lines 1 and 2 come? Explain in your own words those two lines.
7. List one outstanding woman of the world (alive or dead) in each of the following headings:
   1 Queens or Empresses 2 Women Presidents 3 First ten Women Prime Ministers 4 Women Governors General 5 Outstanding women scientists (Nobel Prize winners in science) 6 Women Astronauts or Cosmonauts
8. What was an achievement under the leadership of Elizabeth1, Thatcher, Victoria and Boadicea?
9. Give at least two reasons not mentioned in the poem why you agree with the poet that "women's actions can affect families in every way."
10. Give the meanings of the words or phrases or clauses, which follow, as they are used in the poem. 1 asset 2 aplenty 3 her regal soul of dignity 4 . . . actions . . . affect families in every way 5 took up the mantle 6 influence 7 a source of stability 8 prudent capability 9 at the . . . first chance 10 time immemorial 11 in bellicose negotiations 12 rooting for war 13 in . . . trying times 14 let caution dictate 15 in times of grave danger 16 . . . acted boldly,

not with trepidation 17 floundered 18 . . . ought to applaud . . .
strides 19 in all fields of endeavor 20 dowry 21 to stave off 22
downsize 23 not a single stitch 24 her regal soul of dignity

11. Identify the world's first ten prime ministers.

26. Women Deserve It

'Twas on September 20 in the year nineteen seventy and three
That Billie Jean King taught a lesson to ole "pompous" Bobby
He had defeated Maggie Court calendar grand slam winner
With consummate ease as if she were a minor tennis player
Having won the "Mother's Day Massacre" in that same year
He was sure he would crush Billy Jean; he didn't have a care
Although he was older with his skills clearly in decline
He still saw female players as pretenders to the big time
The Wimbledon champion and joint number one in the forties
Felt at fifty five, he was superior and could whip all the ladies
But Billie Jean cleaned his clock; she did trounce him that day
Before millions around the world, including those in the USA
On that day he was outplayed and humiliated indeed
For daring to suggest women were of an inferior breed
Mr. Bobby Riggs' infernal pride did suffer a terrible blow
He was so completely embarrassed and brought really low
He ought to have known that time really does lessen one's skill
Leaving any player at the mercy of anyone with gargantuan will
It is true that many a hardworking champion of any gender
On a given day might beat a feeble male number one player
The result was that "chauvinist" with the loudest mouth
Was brought to his senses of that there was never a doubt
To think that "Bobby the great" did not even win a set
Against that Ladbrokes and Las Vegas would have bet
While that was the surprise on that day for all and sundry
Who supported Billie Jean King who opposed the insanity
Of limiting a group, encouraging sex discrimination,
As there were a few men totally against equalization,
Ignoring the fact that women must get their due to be free
To work hard to pursue any dream, in this land of liberty
Truth be told at that time even the present harshest critic
Of gender equality would have agreed women deserve it

Answer the questions based on this poem, **Women Deserve It**

1. Research Billy Jean King and Bobby Riggs. What is the context of this poem?
2. Why was it important for Billy Jean to do well?
3. Why were people in 1973 surprised at the performance of Bobby Riggs?
4. What is a grand slam winner? In what sports are there grand slams? Research and find the names of people who won calendar grand slams. Write down the names of those who won at least four in a row.
5. Compare the role of Joan of Arc to Billy Jean. Would Joan of Arc have been honored if she were alive today? Why? Why not?
6. In what way did the happenings in this poem affect the wider society?
7. What other match between a man and a woman is referred to in the poem? Research it and state when it took place, who were involved, and what the result was.
8. If you had to choose the gender of this poet, what would it be and why?
9. Give at least one statement the poet makes of both women and men of that time.
10. In the poem, why do you think Bobby was called "pompous" and "chauvinist"?
11. What do the words "sex discrimination" and "equalization" suggest? Read the poem again and suggest your answers.
12. What does each phrase or clause mean as used in the poem? 1. B defeated M with consummate ease. 2. He would . . . crush BJ. 3 He didn't have a care. 4. He was older with his skills . . . in decline. 5. He saw female players as pretenders to the big time. 6. She did trounce him that day. 7. He was outplayed and humiliated. 8. Women were of an inferior breed. 9. BR's pride did suffer a terrible blow. 10. He was brought really low. 11. Leaving a player at the mercy of one with gargantuan will 12 that chauvinist with the loudest mouth 13 was brought to his senses 14. BJ cleaned his clock. 15 for all and sundry 16 limiting a group 17 women must get their due

27. For Joan of Arc

At just around about six hundred years ago
Joan of Arc was born as you ought to know
A weaver and watcher of her father's flocks
She wanted France freed from British locks
In fourteen hundred twenty and eight
She did set forth a quest to undertake
To change the course of the Hundred Years War
She led from the front nothing did she let her bar
As someone not schooled in the classics or civility
A military neophyte who hated bloodshed was she
Yet the army group she led she went so boldly before
Carried by an unseen hand and absolutely nothing more
Engrossed in luminosity supernaturally she led
As her enemies cowered and were full of dread
The devil's spawn they claimed that she had to be
Yet she was humble and cared about a dead enemy
Betrayed, to her enemy, the British, she was sold
And burned at the stake just as in the days of old
As they killed her some jeered a girl of nineteen
That in fourteen fifty had her guilt wiped clean
Canonized as a saint in nineteen hundred and twenty
Joan of Arc is an example to women eight or eighty
Women of varying beliefs, different times or places
Revere this girl of the ancients with no noble graces
Is she the symbol feminists or women's libs needed?
Or does she stand out because to her call she heeded?
Was she sick? From where did she get her inspiration?
No one ever had a clear answer in any generation.

Answer the following questions based on the poem, **Joan of Arc**.

1. In a paragraph of around 30-40 words state the facts that the poet gives about Joan of Arc.
2. According to the poem when was Joan most famous and why?
3. What three things stand out about Joan of Arc during her time as a warrior?

4. How did Joan's life end? Why?
5. Write your answers to the four questions at the end of the poem using the poem or research. Give reasons for your answers to these questions which are here: 1. Is she the symbol feminists and women's liberation needed? 2. Does she stand out because to her call she heeded? 3. Was she sick? 4. From where did she get her inspiration?
6. According to the poem how was Joan of Arc's dignity restored?
7. Give the meaning of each of the following words as used in the passage:(i) ought (ii)quest (iii) classics (iv)engrossed (v)cowered (vi) spawn (vii) jeered (viii) varying (ix) graces (x) symbol (xi) inspiration
8. In the poem certain clauses or phrases are underlined. Give what you think those clauses or phrases mean. 1led from the front 2 schooled in the classics or civility 3 a military neophyte 4 She was burned at the stake. 5 in fourteen fifty had her guilt wiped clean 6 this girl of the ancients with no noble graces 7 women's liberation 8 her call she heeded

28. For Steven Paul Jobs

Steven Paul Jobs came into the world in 1955
That time none knew how that life would thrive
Enabling our world he always did in many a varied way
Very technologically inventive he was from day to day
Enlarging our borders in his own inimitable style
Nineteen seventy six Apple came out of that pile
Point to iTunes first if you must
Apple's iPods were ones to trust
Unique the iPad is definitely still indeed
Lots will argue an iPhone fills your need
Just imagine what Jobs later could have done too
Over and above expectations, something just new
But before we did know what next from Jobs we would save
Suddenly in October 2011 at 56 **Steve Jobs** was in his grave

Answer all questions based on the acrostic poem, **Steven Paul Jobs**

1. List the products linked to Steve Jobs.
2. Add years to the products linked to Jobs in the poem.
3. Write an orderly timeline for Jobs' life. Begin with his birth, end with his death. State his achievements over time.
4. Why does the poet give the impression of expectation with Jobs' work?
5. Write a paragraph of about 7-10 sentences summarizing the poet's account on Steven Jobs.
6. Give the meaning of the words or phrases as used in the poem. 1 thrive 2 in many a varied way 3 technologically inventive 4 in inimitable style 5 over and above expectations 6. fills your need 7 enlarging our borders 8 unique 9 enabling our world
7. State in your own words what you think the poet means by the last four lines.

Honoring Mothers

29. Mother's Day, some history

From ancient times, that is, from antiquity
Motherhood was always revered in society
Isis honored by the Egyptians and the Romans for some time too
With Horus in her arms foreshadowed the virgin and son tableau
Then Cybele and Rhea that were first of Grecian fame
Held sway in European culture: each a Maternal Dame
Thus in March and April celebrations were much in order
As Romans led the way in celebrating "The Great Mother"
So then it means that when Christianity took pride of place
People transferred honor to the "Virgin Mary, full of Grace"
In the 17th century, "Mothering Day" became the norm
Lasted for a while but the American settlers it did spurn
For neither did time nor their Puritan beliefs allow it
And secular observance with their ideals did conflict
1868 thinking of reuniting families scattered near and far
"Mother Friendship Day" was to fix gaps of the Civil War
In 1870 Julia Howe proposed an "International Mother's Day"
Hoping celebrating Mother would bring peace even far away
In London and Paris she read her Manifesto for Peace
Believing that that 1872 idea can cause a war freeze
In 1873, 18 cities joined 'Mother's Day for Peace' June 2 cause
When funds froze, by 1883, only Boston's honors had no pause
But the Jarvises, daughter and mom, decided in their own way
To cajole, encourage and petition for an official Mother's Day
White for those asleep, pink or red carnations for those alive
Over time the Mother's Day celebrations definitely did thrive
The Jarvis felt they had a very good reason to honor moms in season
So they persevered and in West Virginia they honored moms in 1907
Thus 1909 others too wanted to honor Mothers come-what-may
So 46 states, Canada and Mexico had services for Mother's Day
Then with the World Sunday School Association on her side
Anna Jarvis's push did make a wonderfully significant stride
In 1912, West Virginia first hailed moms in a very official way
And in 1914, President Wilson decided the 2nd Sunday in May
Definitely deserved to be nationally observed as Mother's Day
From then this celebration of mother the world has embraced

Even though the real significance of the day has been debased
By commercialization to an outlandishly astonishing degree
As corporations discovered new ways to mint their solvency
Yet despite what people and businesses do every spring
"Mother's Day" will forever have to it a wonderful ring

Answer the following questions based on the poem, **Mother's Day, some history.**

1. Refer to the three "goddesses" mentioned in the first six lines of the poem and state what it suggests about the countries where they were honored.
2. (a) Which "goddess" had her honor transferred to someone else? (b) Why?
3. (a) What was the seventeenth century celebration so unacceptable to the American settlers that they refused to celebrate it? (b) Give the poet's reasons for the settlers' actions.
4. (a) What was Julia Ward Howe's claim to fame (known for)? (b) What was she hoping to celebrate in the last half of the 19th century and why?
5. (a) What affected Ward Howe's celebrations in the second half of the 19th century? (b) How do you know all places were not affected?
6. Research the following: Isis and Horus and Cybele and Rhea and say what this poem tell you about these four.
7. The poem mentions "Mothering Day" and "International Mother's Day." (a) What were the purported intentions for these two days? (b) Why were these suggestions worthwhile?
8. Using information from the poem alone, write about the contribution made by the Jarvises to what eventually became known as "Mother's Day"?
9. Write a timeline for the history of Mother's Day beginning with **The 17th Century—2nd Sunday May 1914 (The First Mother's Day)**
10. Vocabulary: Write words, phrases or even clauses or sentences that give the meaning or nearly the meaning of the words, phrases or clauses that are numbered. 1 ancient times 2 in antiquity 3 Motherhood was always revered in society 4 held sway in European culture 5 celebrations were in order 6 Christianity took pride

of place 7 transferred the honor 8 Isis, with Horus in her arms foreshadowed the virgin and son tableau 9 Over time Mother's Day celebrations did definitely thrive 10 became the norm 11 America settlers did it spurn 12 Secular observances with their ideals did conflict 13 Reuniting families scattered near and far 14 She penned the Battle Hymn of the Republic 15 it was politic 16 joined in Julia Ward Howe's cause 17 to cajole, encourage and petition 18 Anna Jarvis's push made a wonderfully significant stride 19 Virginia first hailed moms in an official way 20 This celebration of mother the world has embraced 21 The real significance of the day has been debased by commercialization to an outlandishly astonishing degree 22 Corporations discovered a new way to mint their solvency

30. Happy Mother's Day

How wonderful mothers have been for years
Assisting the children despite so many fears
Presenting the guiding hand that's true
Posing no danger to them as they grew
Yearning to share love with them each day
Making them value goodness along the way
Offering shoulders as the places to cry on
Taking time to love at both night or morn
Helping to make each moment one to enjoy
Even when tears overwhelm or pains annoy
Relief you bring when it is needed the most
'Tis the gift that on you Nature has imposed
So days, weeks, months or years will not dim those gifts you see
Do what they may laws don't stop a child from saying "Mommy"
As the rainbow's in the sky and seed-time and harvest go on by
You'll continue to be the world's treasure despite every sad sigh
Happy Mother's Day from all your friends who are as Happy as I

Read the poem **Happy Mother's Day** and answer these questions based on it.

1. Do you think 'Mother's Day' is necessary? Why? Why not?
2. What do you notice, in this poem, about the writer's style?
3. Give three references to point out the poet's feelings about mothers.
4. The poet gives a picture of "A Day in the Life of a Mother." Draft out such his day for her.
5. Give reasons why this poem could be sent to any mother.
6. What do these words mean? 1 yearning 2 overwhelm 3 relief 4 imposed 5 treasure 6 despite 7 sigh
7. What is the color of the rainbow?
8. In your own words explain what the poet means by the following line: "As long as the rainbow stands in the sky and seed-time and harvest go steadily by"

31. To Honor Chestnut and Gibson (The martyrs killed at the Capitol)

Stanza 1
All bullets are clearly colorblind; they have no eye
They forced Chestnut's and Gibson's souls to fly
The dastardly deadly metals killed that foolish lie
That claims skin color says you are better than I

Stanza 2
Bullets aren't prejudiced when directed by those filled with hate
They'll roar with malevolence; they'll hurry folks to the pearly gate
They'll never ask for extra time; they'll never say, "Pray, let's wait,
We must be sure of the hue of each noggin, the color of each pate.

Stanza 3
Bullets won't care that you're black; they won't care if one's white
If propelled by any maniac, they can hurt people with fatal might
They'll pierce every cloak of sanctity; they'll destroy good and right
They'll kill all loveliness there was and turn all joy to eternal night

Answer all questions based on the poem, **To honor Chestnut and Gibson**

1. In between 2-3 sentences, write what the poem states about Chestnut and Gibson.
2. What is the poet's main point in Stanza 1? What is the universal observation he makes?
3. What is the poet's main point in Stanza 2? Why should people not be prejudiced?
4. Explain lines 3 and 4 (the first two lines of Stanza 2). What's "the pearly gate"?
5. In what way does the poet underscore the theme of equality? What does the poet mean when he says bullets never say "must be sure of the hue of each noggin the color of each pate." Firstly, explain the meaning of the quotation. Secondly, give the meaning of each word 1 hue 2 noggin 3 pate
6. Explain what the poet means in Stanza 3. As far as possible give the meaning of the following words as used in the poem: 1 colorblind 2 prejudiced 3 directed 4 malevolence 5 propelled 6 maniac **7** pierce all cloak

32. Is the verdict right? (To honor the Innocence Project)

When the ex-NFLer was freed of the "Murder of The Century"
A media craze fueled outrage against that "incompetent" jury
Before then some people, despite how innocent they might be
Very often had such infinitesimal a chance to be really set free
Especially if black or a minority with little or simply no money
They could afford no high-priced lawyer; few could pay his fee
Some feel doomed to lose thinking their fate is all but sealed
As the rich or famous find justice of which few still dreamed
But for that ex-football player things were not too bad
He did possess that fee plus a fine defense team he had
The world saw the case as it was played out in the public domain
The Defense outmaneuvered the Prosecution to the NFLer's gain
Questions did arise about the investigators' strategy at that time
Whether it ensured the defendant's being set free for that crime
For centuries the question has been, "What should the penalty be
For a murder accused who is found by the jury to be really guilty?"
Should that person, after an appeal, be summarily executed?
Should he simply languish in jail once he's been convicted?
For many, an eye for an eye shows true justice at its best
Except that today justice hasn't always passed every test
Many argue that if proper investigative work is really done
Many more would be free, not in a dark hole but in the sun
Before they joined the defense, two lawyers from the NFLer's case
Had been seeking freedom for the "wrongly accused" of every race
Through The Innocence Project they founded freedom they wrought
For myriads of "convicts" with new hope because of what IP sought
From their non-profit legal clinic, their team worked with great zeal
Due to their investigative work, many decisions judges had to repeal
For poor clients, little cared for, forgotten, without legal avenues left
Saw the IP as their only hope for freedom of which they were bereft
Varied research concluded that many those courts often convicted
Were not only unfairly treated but generally very poorly defended
The IP rid death row of many who were wrongly accused
By unscrupulous law officers who made them the abused
IP found improper testimonies that did secure false convictions

Misconduct and misidentifications that demanded interdictions
Started in the year nineteen hundred ninety and two
IP has such a meaningful record for anyone to view
By 2013, three eleven post conviction DNA exonerations
Point to exceptional work done whatever those assertions
Exonerees did serve an average of thirteen plus years in jail
Seventy percent minorities: a number quite beyond the pale
In over thirty six states the truth was definitely shown
For forty percent of cases, the perp's DNA was known
In the world over, scientific advancement made such change
So that clinical crime scene investigation rightly came of age
Circumstantial evidence's corroboration won't always be in doubt
If the defendants "didn't do it" claims are constructively sorted out
When a murder verdict comes in and a defendant is found "guilty"
Was there ample evidence to prove the accused was not truly free?
Still it is true and very true that the Justice System can't be complacent
For even with doubt none can be always sure if one is guilty or innocent
Yet the Innocent Project's sterling work has truly taken things that far
For poorer and minority defendants to believe that cases are all on par

Answer all questions based on the poem, **Is the verdict right? (To honor the Innocence Project).**

1. Why does this poem demand that the reader think about the guilt or innocence of an accused?
2. What was the "Murder of The Century"? In two or three sentences say what the case was all about?
3. Why does the writer use "quotation marks" to enclose 1 Murder of The Century 2 incompetent 3 wrongly accused 4 convicts 5 lying defendants 6 guilty?
4. Why is it that some defendants have greater difficulties than others?
5. Give some facts the poet gives about the Innocence Project.
6. What is one of the major strengths of the work of the Innocence Project?
7. Give two of the poems' reasons for false convictions.
8. Using information from the poem write a paragraph on the work of the IP.
9. Find words from the poem that mean the same as these words: 1 secured 2 denied 3 effect 4 progress 5 minute 6 overturn 7 too

understanding 8 heightened 9 methods 10 great 11 a variety of 12 animosity 13 not well 14 suffer long 15 after

10. What is the difference between "circumstantial evidence" and "factual evidence"?
11. What is **the perp, death row, varied research?**
12. Explain **summarily executed, languish forever, an eye for an eye.**
13. In what way can the Justice system be complacent? How can that complacency end?
14. What suggestions are made by the poet in his claim that **today justice has not always passed the test?**

SPORTS and POLITICS

33. January Notes

New Year's Day has much history that many can't believe
It was when Rio de Janeiro the Portuguese did conceive
Also 'twas on that day that Castro Batista did overthrow
And Lincoln proclaimed slaves' freedom as we do know
On that day 26 countries the UN declaration did sign
And Australia that day was founded in the southern clime
In other days of January different things took place
Alaska in January among the states did find grace
In this month Nellie Tayloe Ross made history
As the first female governor, hers was a great story
In January, Pol Pot gave Cambodia, Kampuchea as its name
In France, De Gaulle the 1ˢᵗ president of the 5ᵗʰ Republic became
America's 1ˢᵗ bank, the Bank of North America, its business began
The 11ᵗʰ amendment was ratified to safeguard states as much as it can
1066 January 6, Harold II became the last of the Anglo-Saxon kings
He fell to William the Conqueror Oct1066 at the Battle of Hastings
Some GOP House Reps on January 7, 1999
Sought Bill Clinton's presidency to undermine
Basing charges on moral legality
They impeached the president so definitively
Even as some were equally guilty of moral chicanery
This first impeachment trial in 130 years
Underscored American cynicism with all of its fears
17 years before on January 8, in nineteen eighty and two
AT & T had to give up companies in number twenty and two
To ensure that the United States of America could retain its reputation
As a place where the telephone system did have competition
In the past January did give a boost to transportation
1863 London's underground ran between Farringdon and Paddington
Whether we like it or not this is only part of the story
Of world events that occurred in the month of January

Answer the following questions based on the poem, **January Notes**.

1. **Vocabulary**: Give the meanings of these words or phrases as used in the poem, **January Notes: 1** conceive **2** proclaimed **3** founded

4 ratified 5 undermine 6 chicanery 7 cynicism 8 retain 9 boost 10 ethical 11 overthrow 12 underground 13 clime 14 too 15 ought to 16 events

2. From the poem name different things, in topic form, that happened on "New Year's Day." For example, the Founding of a city (Rio de Janeiro)

3. Write from the poem a timeline for January: Day of event, year of event—using only the incidents referred to in the poem. Choose all events that fit any day used in the poem.

4. In alphabetical order, list the names of eight countries referred to in this poem.

5. (a) Name the nine political leaders mentioned in the poem. (b)State where they were leaders and what made them well known.

6. (a) Who was the American President impeached before President Clinton? (b) Find reasons for his impeachment.

7. Using a reference from the program, state why the poet might have been offended at President Clinton's impeachment.

8. (a)Why was AT & T taken to task? (b) Why do you think this is a good or bad way to deal with companies?

34. Cold War Thoughts

When Tsar Nicholas lost his throne
The Russian Revolution set the tone
For a new world order
And a path to power
Not based on royalty
But economic theory
Both the World Wars: One and Two
Did naught to stem worldwide view
That colonialism's grip was all but o'er
As nationalism's effect began to soar
In India, Africa, the world over: everywhere,
Just about all political leaders became aware
That their nation's wealth was theirs to use
Not for a foreign entity to control or abuse
Because of that, both East and West constantly used their might
To influence the leaders of various countries to go Left or Right
But some formally resisted that theoretical bind
And dared to say their nations were Non-Aligned
The leaders: Tito, Sukarno, Nasser, Nkrumah and Nehru
Tried dealing sensibly with both East and West. 'Tis true
Despite all that, in many developing countries civil wars began
For both East and West supported their theoreticians as a plan
To keep national parties of one side or the other really off balance
While they strove continually to get only their systems to advance
These powers sought consistently to widen their own theoretical pool
And never moved from the old proven pattern called "divide and rule"
They preferred one over the other by coups, arms-funding, any means
Destroyed nations' self-determination or curtailed progressive dreams
That act did bode ill for Patrice Lumumba and Abubakar Tafewa Balewa
Ghana, Guinea, Kenya, Tanzania, Uganda, Zambia or the Horn of Africa
At that time Chile and some other countries in South America knew
That the very influence of East or West might cause real havoc too
Brazil, Ecuador, Guyana, Paraguay, Peru, Suriname and Venezuela
Were as politically challenged as Uruguay, Nicaragua and Bolivia
So as the Cold War pace continued in no distinctive form or fancy
The national political parties had distinctive views of democracy

Comparing capitalism and socialism for the good of their country
To ensure their nations progressed economically and politically
Yet civil wars and coup d'états in some countries went on as the norm
When against many dictators, citizens continuously kicked up a storm
Resulting in more devastations and political assassinations
Fomenting more civil wars instead of more reconciliations
Then President Ronald Reagan upped the ante in the arms race free for all
Gorbachev's 'perestroika' and 'glasnost' speeded up the Berlin wall's fall
When Yeltsin refused to use Russian troops to quell revolutionary change
Communism's death knell sounded: then USSR came off the world stage
The Soviet Union did morph from one country into different states
So its former Eastern European Satellites also redefined their fates
Eurasian countries include Belarus, Armenia, and Kazakhstan
Ukraine, Slovenia, Slovakia, Moldova, Latvia and Uzbekistan
Turkmenistan, Tajikistan, Kyrgyzstan, Ingushetia and Estonia
Chechen Republic known too as Chechnya, Lithuania, Serbia
Stavropol Krai and North Ossetia-Alania; and there's Georgia
Also Czech Republic, Bosnia Herzegovina, and Macedonia
To these add Azerbaijan, Kosovo and Dagestan and Russia
Thus the cold war ended and interesting changes came
Alliances were restructured; few things were the same
Russia filled the void left by the old Soviet Empire
USA did hold on to Number1 to which it did aspire
Regional relationships for economic goals abound
Floundering steadily when leadership's not sound
Apartheid, under assault, died and De Klerk set Mandela free
The Cold War thawed; each country eyed its national identity
And neighboring countries consolidated every regional entity
The World became more of a Global Village; that none can ever deny
Though with the Cold War's end Terrorism's threat none can quantify

Answer all questions based on the poem, <u>Cold War Thoughts.</u>

1. What did the poet say was the major change after the overthrow of Tsar Nicholas?
2. What did the poet suggest caused the end of colonialism?
3. Explain the poet's suggestion about 'Nationalism'?
4. Why do you think it was difficult not to be Left or Right?

5. What do you think the word "Non-aligned" mean in the context of the poem?
6. Why were there civil wars in developing countries? (Give at least two different reasons from the poem?
7. (a) Who were Tito, Sukarno, Nasser, Nkrumah and Nehru? (b) Why did they decide to be non-aligned?
8. (a) In the reference to South America, there are three countries that have a special similarity. Name the three countries with that similarity. (b) State the similarity and explain your answer.
9. Explain this quotation from the poem, <u>Cold War Thoughts.</u> "Then President Ronald Reagan upped the ante in the arms race free for all, Gorbachev's 'perestroika' and 'glasnost' speeded up the Berlin wall's fall." Make sure in the explanation to say what is meant by 'perestroika' and 'glasnost.'
10. What did the poet say was Yeltsin's accomplishment?
11. According to the poem, how many Eastern European countries or states were connected to the USSR?
12. State 4 significant things that happened when the Cold War finally ended?
13. **Vocabulary**: Give the meanings of these words or phrases: 1lost his throne 2 naught 3 set the tone 4 a path to power 5 based on 6 to stem view 7 colonialism's grip 8 despite that 9 to keep off balance 10 curtailing progressive dreams 11 bode well 12 they strove to get their systems to advance 13 the norm 14 cause havoc 15 distinctive views 16 self-determination 17 kicked up a storm 18 to quell 19 void 20 fomenting more civil 21 alliances 22 restructured 23 aspire 24 abound 25 floundering 26 under assault 27 thawed 28 consolidated 29 entity 30 leadership's not sound 31 deny 32 threat 33 quantify

35. The World of Sports

The world of sports has changed over time
For many racist rules continued to decline
And those graced with skill continually played
When Apartheid and segregation were derailed
As varied as games have eternally been
The cream of the crop are always seen
In Golf, Cricket, Boxing, Basketball, Rugby or Baseball
NASCAR, Grand Prix, Formula One, Polo or Football
The greats now and ever have always come to the fore
As if those who follow sports couldn't aspire for more
There will forever be a long list of people we must hail
Those who've shown skill consistently and without fail
Exploits they have performed breathtakingly supreme
Captivating audiences, mesmerized in an eternal dream
Their standards high, their deeds unmatched
They left most speechless while they watched
Time could not rob them of their glory
And their exploits told a singular story
Emile Zatopek an Olympic great of enduring fame
Like Owens, Lewis and Bolt, in track, made a name
As Quarrie, Crawford, Johnson, Coe and Alberto Juantorena
Kipchonge Keino of Kenya and from Ethiopia, Abebe Bikila
Who unbowed by the crippling results of accident's devastating decree
Excelled in both Paralympics archery and Norwegian dogsled mastery
There's little doubt that sports does have an appeal none can deny
For in many nations of the world Olympic sports people do unify
In the drink Spitz was surpassed by Phelps who also made his mark
Yet wintry weather brought out many of those did not need a spark
Watson, Hašek, Selänne, Samuelsson, Koivu, Helminen, Crosby
Wickenheiser, White, Ruggiero, Ovechkin, Kharlamov, Gretzky
Witt, Vonn, Thomas, Davis, Datsyuk, Bure, Bubník, Bonaly
Wanted to win so they'd be a part of Winter Olympic revelry

No question sports the world over linked people disparate
Sports fueled competition and silenced drumbeats of hate
So that the Jims: Thorpe and Brown, reached heights in the NFL

As did Brady, Butkus, White and the others too numerous to tell
While in the United States Super-Bowl Sunday has its own charm
When some states are cold outside; inside thrill keeps hearts warm
In the NFL, there are the Lions, Rams, Redskins, Saints and Steelers
The Vikings, Titans, Texans, Seahawks, Ravens, Patriots and Raiders
The Bears, Bengals, Bills, Broncos, Browns, Buccaneers and Chargers
Cardinals, Colts, Cowboys, Dolphins, Jaguars, Jets and Packers
Chiefs, Eagles, Falcons, the Forty Niners, Giants and Panthers
In a game where hands are used more oft than the feet
The name "football" is definitely not quite so very neat
As "The Beautiful Game" demands sleight of foot to do the trick
To perfect the feint, the pass and then bend that "bicycle kick"
Reminds one of FIFA's past World Cup greats
In that their skills defied their very different gaits
Beckenbauer, Pele, Zico, Zidane, Eusebio, Gerson or Nakata
Would have enjoyed Celtics or United or Real or Ajax or Barcelona
Just as Rijkaard, Socrates, Milla, Beckham, Garrincha or Maldini
Might have happily joined Diego Maradona and played for Napoli
The cousin of association football, Rugby is quite unique
And as a game it provides many with new heights to seek
O'Driscoll, Montgomery, Campese, Wilkinson and Lomu
All world cup glory for their nations did pursue
Still there are other games that many do enthrall
One such is the game that's called baseball
It has an American claimed formation that's very thin
For the game was before written about by Jane Austen
That raised doubts about its "American Introduction"
As Northanger Abbey belied the American invention
Baseball boasts a talented list that is long indeed
As quite many in that game truly did succeed
But PEDs have truncated the list at best
Honor's left to past greats who passed the acid test
Aaron, Mays, Ruth, DiMaggio, Koufax, Yogi Berra
Robinson, Ripken, Clemente, Gehrig, Young and Rivera
Baseball's cousin, cricket, has its own international structure
With 104 member countries cricket continues to prosper
Its competitions are varied and give cause for intrigue
Especially with the shortest format the T20 League
In "The Gentleman's Game" for years all did agree

Don Bradman was the best batsman of any country
Yet over time for their sheer skill and longevity
Tendulkar and Lara closed the gap considerably
Lara's four and five hundred lead records for batting
But many leaders there've been in the art of bowling
While Muralitharan and Warne do have the numbers
Thommo, Lillee, "Whispering Death" flayed "the Timbers"
Sobers might arguably go down as the best all-rounder
And Viv Richards for the title of Best One-day player
In the latest version of the game there is clearly no doubt
In T20 batting Gayle, Kohli or Mac Callum might win in a rout
In ATP and WTA tennis there is little argument, no debating
The best players are known; they dominate the ranking
Only seven men have ever won all four slams at all
Perry, Budge, Laver, Emerson, Agassi, Federer and Nadal
The women's game is equally indeed quite fascinating
Despite constant preparing only few won all slams after trying
They are Connolly, Hart, Fry, Court, King, Evert and Navratilova
In addition to Steffi Graf, Serena Williams and Maria Sharapova
There is also "The Sport of Kings" for everyone to savor indeed
Both English and US Triple Crowns attract owners of many a steed
The 2000 Guineas, Epsom Derby and St. Leger can attract any chap
As would The Kentucky Derby, Preakness Stakes and Belmont Handicap
Lester Piggott was the last rider to win the English Triple Crown
In the US Steve Cauthen had done the same; in 1978 he had won
Some other sports have made for many bucket loads of money
Auto racing, Golf, Boxing, Basketball produced rich folks a plenty
Earnhardt, the Black Knight, Ali, Air Jordan, Marciano, Mayweather
Moss, the Squire, Klitscko, Magic, Pacquiao, the Hawk, Bird, Tiger
Andretti, the Golden Bear, Foreman, the Dream, Louis, Schumacher
Show forever that though sports might vary we enjoy it together
"The Sweet Science" gave so many people a future full of hope
Like Tyson and De La Hoya others used their skills to cope
Rounders, Squash, Badminton, Netball are games many play too
But their numbers in comparison to other sports are fairly few
Still whatever we may like about our sport or game
Giving our very best in it is what makes us all the same

Answer all questions based on the poem, <u>The World of Sports</u>

1. Why did sporting situations change?
2. At least two things the poet says sports do are

    1_____

    2_____

3. Origins of sports or games have rarely been controversial. In this poem which sport's national origin is under question? Why?
4. When you read the writer's verses on sports, what is his opinion about football? Why would you agree or disagree with him?
5. In the account about Olympic athletes, the poet mentions Abele Bikila. Write in two or three sentences what the writer says about Bikila.
6. According to the poem, how many teams are in the NFL?
7. What are the English Triple Crown and the US Triple Crown?
8. Who are the jockeys to have last won the English and US Triple crowns? State 1 Name of horse 2 Name of jockey 3 Year the Triple Crown was won. 4. Name of the trainer of the horse.

Year of Last English Triple Crown winner	Name of Horse	Name of Jockey	Name of Trainer

Year of Last US Triple Crown winner	Name of Horse	Name of Jockey	Name of Trainer

9. Give any reason from the poem for the poet's apparent problem in naming the best Baseball players.
10. The poet used phrases to refer to different sports. What sport does each phrase refer to?

Nickname	Sport
The Sweet Science	
The Sport of Kings	
The Gentleman's game	

The Beautiful Game	

11. In the poem there are references to five of the best golfers ever by their nicknames.

Name the five.

Nickname	Golfer

12. Vocabulary: Give the meaning of these words, phrases, clauses or sentences as used in the poem, The World of Sports 1 segregation ways were derailed 2 the cream of the crop seen 3 graced with skill 4 aspire for more 5 exploits tell their story 6 unbowed 7 always come to the fore 8 made his mark 9 deeds unmatched 10 sleight of foot to do the trick 11 to perfect the feint 12 win in a rout 13 crippling results of accident's devastating decree 14 truncated the list 15 different gaits 16 its American introduction 17 Time cannot rob them of their glory 18 used their skills to cope 19 their skill and longevity 20 silent drumbeats of hate 21 in the drink

13. Use the poem to list these groups: 1 Olympic track stars 2 Olympic swimmers 3 Hockey players 4 Cricketers 5 Boxers 6 Jockeys 7 Female Winter Olympic athletes 8 NFL players 9 Male tennis Players 10 Basketball Players 11 Baseball players 12 Female tennis players 13 Rugby players 14 FIFA Football or Soccer players

14. Why do you think the following words are placed in quotation marks? 1 football 2 the beautiful game 3 Bicycle kick 4 American Introduction 5 Whispering Death 6 the Timbers 7 The Sport of Kings 8 the Sweet Science

15. From the poem, pick out, if possible, examples of antonyms and homonyms.

16. Which word used in the poem can readily refer to actions in both boxing and FIFA Football (Soccer)?

36. A Memorable Match

Confidently
With pugilistic sweetness that defied the long odds
He wore his man down
Poof
Slip
Dance
Bob
Weave
In
Out
Hold
Break—Not a float—But with the smartness of him who made the bee-sting famous
He 'tied' the bull-necked rusher
Made his legs freeze
His vaunted jab a non-factor
Fielded him with blows
With gum-shield out
Kept up by the canvas
Willing to give him only its second support
Pride played out,
As idle threats became tasteless
In the convincing whipping
Dealt for real by a fearless opponent
The sockless warrior stood
Clueless
Void of invincibility
Defeated
Humbled; mercifully pitied
That night by a better warrior
Then came the after-shock
Bereft of flamboyance
Stripped of pomp
The beaten, once champ
Of frightened foes
That lost to intimidation

Before the first bell sounded
Begged for a handshake
Groveled in hope of a rematch
He who came to punish
Showed the bumps of punishing blows
As his chastened management
In a most hypocritical show
Showered praise
And heaped kudos
Richly deserved
On the one ten days before
They berated
Castigated
And
Denounced
He who
Defying the odds
Majestically stood
King of pugilistic artistry

Answer questions based on the poem all, A Memorable Match

1. Why do you think the title of this poem is appropriate?
2. List the senses stressed by the poet.
3. Give the poem's 10-12 words that indicate what sport this "match" is about.
4. State the words or phrases the poet used to identify the players in this "Memorable Match."
5. Quote the line in this poem that refers to a famous sports personality.
6. Why was the victor given underdog status?
7. Give the poet's reason why the loser here won many matches in the past.
8. Write in a paragraph of between four to six sentences how the match was won.
9. (a) How was the winner treated by the loser's team before this match took place? (b) Quote words from the poem to support the answers in 7 (a).

10. Why does the poet refer to the management team of the loser as "hypocritical"?
11. (a) What comes to mind when one thinks about a rematch? (b) Who usually wants a rematch?
12. Give the meaning of these words, phrases or clauses as used in the poem: 1 defied 2 vaunted 3 freeze 4 long odds 5 a non-factor 6 support 7 idle threats became tasteless 8 opponent 9 pomp 10 void of invincibility 11 bereft of flamboyance 12 intimidation 13 groveled 14 heaped kudos

37. Assassinations

From time immemorial so it has always been
Humans killed others oft times to achieve a dream
Some for power for the right to use might to ingratiate
And leaders they couldn't influence, they'd assassinate
For the killing of leaders over time was the order of the day
The chosen method to remove those who refused others a say
No thought of what's in a country's or a nation's best interest
Intended to end the life of someone not bending to their behest
Tyrannicide's usually aimed at rending an ending to the will
Of one unprepared to just follow in a particular direction still
Sometimes it's due to envy or people's not wanting to wait
To achieve a prescribed goal they think they earned by fate
Many assassinations have been for personal political gain
As the claimants in patriotic garb their intent would feign
Leaders, like Assyrian King Sennacherib, had their lives taken
By trusted family or friends, part of the group they had chosen
All know of Julius Caesar's demise of which history did tell
And of Roman emperors whom their own protectors did fell
For those Caesars became victims of their own praetorian guards
Who did regard some of those emperors as really powerful frauds
An Italian assassinations' list will number quite so many
Including Aldo Moro, King Umberto 1, and Marco Biagi
Before the Revolution, Russian leaders lost their lives, more than a few
Killed were a tsar, prime minister and from the emperors there were two
The French had two kings and presidents to the great beyond sent
And an assassin ensured William the Silent in 1584 also there went
In time the whole world had its fill of the work of every kind of assassin
Like the ones that dispatched Mohandas Gandhi, Aquino, Sadat, and Rabin
Whether it was a prime minister, king, president, or emperor who was killed
Behind, such a great void is left that for many years it remains so unfulfilled
For like Presidents Abe Lincoln, Garfield, McKinley and John F. Kennedy
Death can deny leaders any chance to complete their agendas satisfactorily
But there was an assassination that went absolutely much too far
Princip's 1914 killing of the Archduke led to the First World War
Yet with the passage of time none can be too sure
Of what kind of a murderous attack is at any door

In the past what mattered was the sniper's skill and artistry
Making him snuff out lives from afar so unceremoniously
But in the 21ˢᵗ century things have changed dramatically
Assassins are very thorough giving up their lives freely
Suicide bombers who ply their trade anyplace, anywhere
Kill with gay abandon contemptuously and without fear
9/11 and Rajiv Gandhi's death underscore their execution
Of the jobs they carry out; they care not about retribution
IEDs or suicide vests mattered not to assassins at all
As long as all perceived enemies made that last call

Read the poem, **Assassinations,** and answer the questions based on it.

1. What does the poet suggest as reasons for assassinations?
2. What is the similarity, if any between the assassinations of Sennacherib and Julius Caesar?
3. Why were some Emperors' guards complicit in their murders?
4. Give the similarity among the French, Italian, and Russian lists.
5. Research the deaths of Aquino, Gandhi, Sadat and Rabin, how were they similar or different?
6. Why does the writer lament the killing of leaders?
7. Who was the Archduke killed and what was the result of his killing?
8. Research and fill out below the names mentioned in the poem. Fill out the required information in the table below.

Victim	Assassin	Where killed	When killed	How killed	Result of killing
King Sennacherib					
Julius Caesar					
Marco Biagi					
P M Aldo Moro					
King Umberto 1					

PM Indira Gandhi					
William the Silent					
Mahatma Gandhi					
Sen. Ben Aquino					
Anwar Sadat					
Yitzhak Rabin					
President Lincoln					
President Garfield					
Pres. Mc Kinley					
President Kennedy					
PM Rajiv Gandhi					
Austrian Archduke Franz Ferdinand					

9. Give the meanings of these words as they are used in the poem. 1 fell 2 ingratiate 3 influence 4 method 5 chance 6 bending 7 rending an ending 8 unprepared to follow 9 prescribed goal 10 demise 11 with gay abandon 12 retribution 13 behest 14 the world had its fill of 15 snuff out lives

10. What is the poet suggesting by the following: a. the claimants in patriotic garb their intent did feign b. the world has had its fill of the work of every kind of assassin c. ply their trade d. their execution of the jobs they carry out

38. GONE

Surreptitiously
Quietly
Hidden bomb
Hidden pistol
Great Planning
Sometimes
Thoughtless
Sudden Action
Booth or Guiteau
Oswald or Czolgosz
Guards or Sycophants
Assumed for Friends
Rather than
Certified as Foes
What does it matter?
The Deed is done
Whether 'twas
Betrayal in March and October
Or much pain in April and May
Or great shock in January and July
Or deep agony in September and December
Or intense slow march in November
Followed by tears: some of extreme sadness
Or others of hidden gleefulness
What does it matter?
The Deed is done.
In death the power was no more
For Louis XVI, Czar Nicholas, or Caesar of yore
Lincoln, Garfield, McKinley, Kennedy
Benazir Bhutto, Indira and Rajiv Gandhi
Like The Mahatma were cut down unceremoniously
Life can end in a whimper
What does it matter?
The Deed is done

Answer the questions based on the poem, **<u>GONE</u>**.

1. What do the people mentioned in the poem all have in common?
2. Affix any names or titles in the poem to any of the months mentioned.
3. Why does the poet write the words "The Deed is done" at those points in the poem?
4. At the beginning of the poem, the poet uses the following words and phrases: Surreptitiously, Quietly, Hidden bomb, Hidden pistol, Great Planning. What does he point out by his using them?
5. Who are "the first four names" mentioned in the poem? To whom is each name linked?
6. Why does the poet use specific suggested actions to the months stated in the poem? Explain: "Great shock in January and July; Betrayal in March and October; Pain in April and May; Agony in September and December;" and "Slow marching in November."
7. What does the writer imply by the two reactions to "tears"? (b) Why can both responses be appropriate?
8. What words or phrases mean nearly the same as the following phrases or words used in the poem? 1 extreme sadness 2 hidden gleefulness 3 cut down unceremoniously 4 life can end in a whimper 5 agony 6 betrayal

39. Exploration and Discovery: The Americas and New World Issues

From earliest times man used a boat
When he realized in it he could float
In the beginning he sailed for revelry
From place to place new sights to see
As he kept travelling from time to time
He wondered if there was another clime
As he wondered he decided to wander too
Looking to unearth any facts that were new
About Antarctica, Europe or Asia
Australia, the Americas or Africa
Or of any of those several New World strands
The Treaty of Tordesillas gave by Papal hands
So centuries later we yearn to learn more
Of the "truth" behind those days of yore
When all mariners traversed from shore to shore
Setting their sights on unknown sites to explore
Portuguese were among leading seafarers some say
Touring by Africa and visiting Zipangu and Cathay
Venetians, Phoenicians and Norsemen travelled too
While Mongoloid tribes found areas that were new
Yet whate'er the truth about discovering America might be
The powers named those continents for Amerigo Vespucci
The Spaniards came first to various coasts of "West India"
And curtailed native numbers in Hispaniola and Jamaica
300,000 Tainos were in Hispaniola in fourteen ninety-two
And showed some clear signs of increasing in numbers too
But one hundred and fifty years later, by sixteen fifty eight
The numbers clearly revealed the Arawaks unfortunate fate
In Hispaniola, less than 500 left—almost total annihilation
In Jamaica, all 60, 000 disappeared—so absolute extinction
Historians claimed the Spaniards removed the natives in style
They used their bloodhounds to exterminate for quite a while.
One dog killed more Arawaks than ten soldiers, people say
They burnt caciques alive in peacetime, didn't need a fray
In fact, others got rid of some for sport, and that is no joke

They did compete to cut off Arawak heads with one stroke
From horseback, at high speed, they ran swords through many
Overworked some, starved others, and beat the rest needlessly
So there in South America is Kaisikaitu, the river of the dead
And the scenes of caciques in their Benabs cowering in dread
And Orinoco and Essequibo just below the reaches of Roraima
Link with Potaro and Cayuni and Mazaruni near to Venezuela
Majestic Kaieteur has Lofty Angel not so far from his side
Both Cascading cataracts supreme, South American pride
The Andean Titicaca that lords over both Bolivia and Peru
Is no less South American than Pampas and Rupununi too
Behold Little England and Helen of the West Indies
Caribs' possessions before Brittania ruled the seas
None can claim that the Caribs surrendered without a fuss
After the West Indian Islands were reached by Columbus
But conquistadors brought the West Indians sadness too
In Mexico, Hispaniola, Jamaica, Watling Island or Peru
Coming without women, wanting their share of gold
They willingly stooped to the most evil nature untold
While Colonial Pilgrims came buttressed by Faith's decree
To find in America a home for all to be free from tyranny
Led by the Dutch sugarcane replaced the plantations of tobacco
Yet Raleigh felt the Guianas had the gold of Manoa's Eldorado
The British, Dutch and French dredged by the banks of rivers
Locals panned there, found their share. Hail the porkknockers
In the early 1990's, on ancestral lands of the Wapishana, Patamona
Arawak, Carib, Akawaio, Warrau, Macushi, Wai-Wai and Arecuna
Whom the colonial masters saw and called the native Amerindians
Gold was found in the Guianas by companies owned by Canadians
Meanwhile in Barbados, stalactites and stalagmites in caves do abound
The many effects of Pelée and Soufrière on some islands still are found
In the early 2000s the island of Montserrat was all aglow
As it and Martinique were affected around a century ago
Reviving memories of what happened in Java and Sumatra
When rice fields were destroyed by Krakatoa and Tambora
For while many still refuse to think about the distant past
None can deny explorations patent truth will forever last
For because of man's insatiable perpetual curiousity
The world has benefited from widespread discovery

Answer all questions based on the poem, <u>New World Thoughts</u>

1. **<u>Vocabulary</u>. Give the meaning of each of the following numbered words or phrases as used in the poem.** 1 revelry 2 perpetual 3 buttressed 4 tyranny 5 dredged 6 insatiable 7 cowering 8 aglow 9 caciques 10 exterminate 11 fray 12 replaced 13 effects 14 unearth 15 strands 16 traversed 17 cataracts 18 clime 19 days of yore 20 abound 21 wander 22 stooped 23 benefited 24 surrendered without a fuss 25 absolute extinction 26 perpetual curiosity 27 discovery 28 patent 29 deny 30 forever 31 untold

2. The poet uses four words that refer to Native Americans who first lived in the West Indies. Give the words as follows: 1. 1 word that refers to both groups 2. 1 word that only refers to 1 group. 3. 2 words that refer to the second group.

3. What reason did the poet give for man's using a boat for the first time?

4. Give other reasons for man's constant travels from place to place?

5. List some of those "mariners" the poet referred to.

6. What are at least two words the poet uses for the early explorers?

7. The poet talks about the "unfortunate fate" of the Arawaks. In one paragraph of 3-5 sentences show how he supports this claim.

8. According to the poet, what were some methods used to eliminate the Tainos or Arawaks.

9. Name at least four volcanoes mentioned in the poem.

10. List at least three islands mentioned in the poem.

11. List two waterfalls and two grasslands also in this poem.

12. Name at least four rivers mentioned in this poem.

13. Explain "The Treaty of Tordesillas."

14. Explain what the poet is talking about in this line, "In the early 2000s the island of Montserrat was all aglow"

15. Explain the poet's understanding of the Pilgrims' coming of the to America.

16. Because this is a poem, state the writer's style. How does he or she make this poem worth reading?

17. What are: 1 Zipangu 2 Cathay 3 Little England 4 Helen of the West Indies 5 Britannia 6 Eldorado 7 the Guianas?

18. Who are: Raleigh, Manoa, Amerigo Vespucci and Columbus?

19. Who are the possible "colonial masters" in this poem?

20. Who were the porkknockers according to the poet? What did they do?